G000268952

Digging in the Dark

To Alison, who has (once again) been the level head in our household whilst the author in the dungeon has managed to escape reality on a regular basis. My skills don't reach far enough to put my love and appreciation into words.

Also, to my Mum, Jacqueline, who has (once again) acted as my proofreader and critic. Your constant help and enthusiastic support have been invaluable.

And to my friend, Trevor Stockbridge, who has (once again) played a huge part in the completion of this book. Your driving and photography skills will always be greatly appreciated.

Finally, thanks to my immediate and extended family, who have shown so much enthusiasm and much-needed moral support since the beginning of my writing career, especially my dad, John, who has added *book seller* to his long list of family duties.

Digging in the Dark

A History of the
Yorkshire Resurrectionists

Ben Johnson

PEN & SWORD
HISTORY

First published in Great Britain in 2017 by
Pen & Sword History
An imprint of
Pen & Sword Books Ltd
47 Church Street
Barnsley
South Yorkshire
S70 2AS

Copyright © Ben Johnson, 2017

ISBN 978 1 47387 817 4

The right of Ben Johnson to be identified as Author of this work has been asserted by him in accordance with the Copyright, Designs and Patents Act 1988.

A CIP catalogue record for this book is
available from the British Library.

All rights reserved. No part of this book may be reproduced or transmitted in any form or by any means, electronic or mechanical including photocopying, recording or by any information storage and retrieval system, without permission from the Publisher in writing.

Typeset in Ehrhardt by
Mac Style Ltd, Bridlington, East Yorkshire

Printed and bound in Malta
By Gutenberg Press Ltd.

Pen & Sword Books Ltd incorporates the Imprints of Pen & Sword Archaeology, Atlas, Aviation, Battleground, Discovery, Family History, History, Maritime, Military, Naval, Politics, Railways, Select, Transport, True Crime, Fiction, Frontline Books, Leo Cooper, Praetorian Press, Seaforth Publishing, Wharncliffe and White Owl.

For a complete list of Pen & Sword titles please contact
PEN & SWORD BOOKS LIMITED
47 Church Street, Barnsley, South Yorkshire, S70 2AS, England
E-mail: enquiries@pen-and-sword.co.uk
Website: www.pen-and-sword.co.uk

Contents

At the sight of that horrible human charnel-house, its fragments of limbs, its grimacing faces and cloven heads, the bloody cesspool in which we walked around, the revolting odour it exhaled, the swarms of sparrows fighting over scraps of lungs, and the rats in the corners gnawing bleeding vertebrae, such a feeling of horror possessed me that I leapt out of the window, and ran panting home as though Death and all his hideous crew were at my heels. I spent twenty-four hours stunned by this first impression, wanting to hear no more talk of anatomy, or dissection, or medicine, and meditating on a thousand mad schemes to extricate myself from the future that menaced me.

Hector Berlioz, French Composer –
on discovering the dissection suite at a medical school

Prologue – Descent into Darkness

'The darker the night, the brighter the stars. The deeper the grief, the closer is God.'

Fyodor Dostoyevsky – Crime and Punishment

The macabre matter of grave-robbing, or body snatching, is something which, thankfully, is rather uncommon in today's world, save for a handful of distasteful acts which occur sporadically in the deep and dark corners of our planet.

The subject itself is one that brings with it a guilty fascination, rather like that which accompanies the reading of a particularly gruesome historic crime report. We know that the words we are processing in our already crowded minds spell out the goriest details of a terrible event, but the passing of time walks hand in hand with a feeling of innocent detachment from the subject in question.

In such cases, we tend to see the victims as names on pages, rather than lives that were tragically lost to acts of unrivalled violence and evil, as we picture the scene in our minds; a distant land we call *the past*, a place which bears no more familiarity to us than the surface of the moon.

We picture dark alleyways and gas lamps, squalid hovels inhabited by toothless, feckless and entirely disposable beings framed by candle-lit rooms and foggy nights. It is no more reality to us than a *Tim Burton* film set, deliberately created to be as grotesque and stylised as our imaginations allow.

Yet, these shadowy beings that either populate the pages of the history books, or have lost their identities to the ravages of time, were just like us. They lived their lives under the same sky, and walked upon the same ground as that which we tread upon today.

Their suffering was as real as their existence, yet throughout our fascination with the macabre and gloomy past, we forget that real tears were shed, real blood spilled, and real lives lost. Perhaps we should spend as much time imagining the feelings of the past as we do picturing the scene and losing ourselves in the altered reality conjured by our own imaginations.

The subject matter for this book is undeniably as dark and gloomy as that of any depraved murder, yet on the face of it, the cases of which you are about to read seem to be missing something extremely important – a victim.

The theft of a body, already declared and interred as no longer living, would seem to indicate a victimless crime; a merely distasteful practice in which the no longer inhabited shell of a former person is traded for a handful of coins, and a chance to perform exploratory procedures which could never have been attempted upon the living.

Yet, we forget that for every cadaver which was to end up being unceremoniously dragged from its final resting place and displayed on the cold, sterile examination slabs of the medical schools, there were families left without a place to mourn, and loved ones robbed of their fond memories of the deceased, with only the uncertainty of what had become of the remains of their parents, lovers and children.

It is with this in mind that I have made every attempt to document the identity of the deceased, in order for their names to live on, as well as those of the people who committed terrible crimes against their defenceless remains, and probably don't deserve to be immortalised in black and white.

There are also, admittedly, certain passages and stories within this compendium which will no doubt illicit a smile from many readers. However, rather than make light of these terrible occurrences (apart from one truly distasteful story title), it is important to tell them as they were, and often, in the depths of despair, come moments of unintentional laughter.

Therefore, while we imagine these terrible, yet fascinating, and sometimes even darkly humorous events, perhaps we should spare a moment to put ourselves in the minds of those who suffered at the hands of the resurrectionists, and remember that their victims were not the dead, but the living.

Introduction – A Cruel Deliverance

'History is a cyclic poem; written by time upon the memories of man.'
Percy Bysshe Shelley – A Defence of Poetry

Part 1 – The Taking of a Thief

As with every subject, there is always a flagship example, one that involves a famous person, or has since evolved into a well known story. Our opening chapter includes both, and tells the tale of a man who was hunted for many years, and continued to be a wanted man, even after his brutal and public execution.

The reason for his earthly remains being so keenly sought after is very different from the reason for which nefarious characters would attack a final resting place with pick and shovel in future years, yet the outcome is the same; an empty coffin, and a dream of riches for those who wielded the offending picks and shovels.

The eighteenth century was a time where religion ruled all, and the society of Britain was held in place by an almost universal servitude to God. However, in this case, the questionable character of the victim seems to have outweighed this ever-present dogma, and allowed for a few hours of digging in the darkness for the forbidden treasure that lay beneath.

The former inhabitant of the empty coffin was none other than the legendary highwayman, Richard 'Dick' Turpin. Having long since terrorised the rural tracks of eighteenth century England, Turpin had finally been apprehended, and, owing to his fearsome reputation, had been victim to a brutal and public execution.

Turpin had been born in Essex, the date being uncertain, but he was baptised on 21 September, 1705. His early years seem to have been fairly normal for a young man at this time, having received a little schooling before joining his father in the family butchery trade. There exist several reports, which claim that the young Turpin was a bright and cheerful young man, who was happy and content in his schooling, and a diligent and hard-worker within the Turpin home and the family business.

However, it was this particular trade that was to cast Turpin towards the criminal lifestyle in which he would remain for the rest of his life. The customers of the family shop were keen to avail themselves with the very best quality meat, and Turpin, by the age of 21, was only too keen to oblige. The unassuming butcher's apprentice took to making long trips during the dark nights, and usually returned by horse and cart, surrounded by a number of sacks, all of which contained the finest quality meat available; the venison, grouse and other delicacies which had, until that evening, been roaming on any number of private estates.

The extra income for the family was much appreciated, and business was booming for Mr Turpin senior, who saw a regular flow of wealthy customers return to his store again and again. Rumour has it that several of these valued customers were actually buying back their own property, skinned and portioned to perfection. Unfortunately, the ease with which he had found a way to make a decent living spurred the younger Turpin onto bigger, and more serious, pastimes and, before long, he had taken several more steps down the ladder into criminality, operating as a burglar, horse thief, and fledgling highwayman.

By the time he reached his mid-twenties, Turpin was the leader of a local gang, who wrought havoc throughout the length and breadth of the country as he travelled upon his horse, Black Bess, robbing and pillaging with his band of brothers, each time managing to make good their escape. A fascinating account of one of the gang's more audacious robberies exists, and was originally published in *Read's Weekly Journal* on 8 February 1735. The story appears below in its entirety:

On Saturday night last, about seven o'clock, five rogues entered the house of the Widow Shelley at Loughton in Essex, having pistols etc. and threatened to murder the old lady if she would not tell them where her money lay, which she obstinately refused for some time, they threatened to lay her across the fire, if she did not instantly tell them, which she would not do.

But her son being in the room, and threatened to be murdered, cried out, he would tell them, if they would not murder his mother, and did, whereupon they went upstairs, and took near £100, a silver tankard, and other plate, and all manner of household goods. They afterwards went into the cellar and drank several bottles of ale and wine, broiled some meat, and ate the relics of a fillet of veal.

While they were doing this, two of their gang went to Mr Turkles, a farmer, who rents one end of the widow's house, and robbed him of above £20 and then they all went off, taking two of the farmer's horses, to carry off their luggage, the horses were found on Sunday the following morning in Old Street, and stayed about three hours in the house.

However, at the age of 30, Turpin's luck finally ran out; he and his gang fell victim to a trap – a stagecoach laden with valuable goods which was being watched every inch of its journey by an unseen militia, ready to pounce upon the gang when the moment of no return had been reached.

Turpin was the only member of the gang to escape, the rest having been easily captured by the militia. Without his gang, and acutely aware that the authorities would stop at nothing to find the escaped highwayman, Turpin disappeared, leaving even his family to wonder what had become of their troublesome offspring. It is suggested that Turpin travelled abroad at this stage, given a number of reported sightings made in the Netherlands. This would certainly make sense, as no sightings of 'Turpin the Butcher' were made in almost two years, until a coach was forcefully halted within the boundaries of Epping Forest.

The two masked highwaymen, who quickly relieved the occupants of their valuables, were Turpin, and an accomplice, Thomas Rowden. Both would go on to commit a number of similar robberies over the next twelve months, until Rowden was convicted of dealing in counterfeit currency and transported to the colonies.

After another brief period of anonymity, Turpin returned to the public eye less than twelve months later. But his fearsome reputation was soon to be propelled even further into infamy, as his name became linked with two deaths, one reported to have been accidental, and the other nothing short of cold-blooded murder.

Turpin had taken to working with two brothers, John and Matthew King but, still in the early days of their working relationship, the group had been tracked down by the militia, who successfully captured John King, who was forced to divulge the location of his brother and the famous Dick Turpin.

During the resulting gunfight, which took place in a wooded area near Whitechapel, London, Matthew King was shot and killed. However, it was claimed by members of the militia that the shot was fired not by themselves, but by Turpin, who had decided that he would stand a better chance of escaping alone and did not wish to leave more witnesses than absolutely necessary.

Although Turpin did make good his escape, it would not be long before things would escalate even further. Having safely made his way to a hideout in Epping Forest, Turpin was spotted by Thomas Morris, a member of the Forest Keepers. Unwisely relying on his own abilities and his two trusty pistols, Morris made the fatal mistake of attempting to tackle Turpin alone. Unfortunately, Morris did not have chance to discharge either of his revolvers because Turpin had seen Morris as he drew nearer and, with lightening speed, killed him with one shot from his carbine. The incident, which included a description of Turpin, was published in the *Gentleman's Magazine* in June, 1737:

> *It having been represented to the King, that Richard Turpin did on Wednesday the 4th of May last, barbarously murder Thomas Morris, Servant to Henry Tomson, one of the Keepers of Epping-Forest, and commit other notorious Felonies and Robberies near London, his Majesty is pleased to promise his most gracious Pardon to any of his Accomplices, and a Reward of £200 to any Person or Persons that shall discover him, so as he may be apprehended and convicted.*
>
> *Turpin was born at Thacksted in Essex, is about Thirty, by Trade a Butcher, about 5 Feet 9 Inches high, brown Complexion, very much mark'd with the Small Pox, his Cheek-bones broad, his Face thinner towards the Bottom, his Visage short, pretty upright, and broad about the Shoulders.*

This was to be the major incident that would send the infamous Turpin careering towards his eventual capture within the countryside of Yorkshire, and begins the fascinating tale of his trial, his execution, and his brief resurrection.

In late June 1737, Turpin arrived in Yorkshire after the last few weeks fleeing from the militia who hunted him relentlessly in London and the Home Counties. Yet, by the time he set foot over the borders of God's own country, it would appear that much of the cunning and bravado for which Turpin had been famed had disappeared, along with his captured colleagues. Adopting the name of 'John Palmer' in order to avail himself with even a slight chance of his true persona remaining a secret, those who were able to recollect his presence in Yorkshire often described 'Palmer' as being listless, depressed, and lacking any sense of social integration.

Whilst staying in Brough, East Yorkshire, Turpin is reported to have been something of a loner, but with a changeable and volatile nature. This was proved correct when, in front of several witnesses, Turpin produced his revolver and shot a neighbour's gamecock in the street. The neighbour, who took exception to this senseless slaying, was similarly threatened with the revolver, at which point the local militia was brought in to remove Turpin from the street and to keep him in their custody until he could be brought before magistrates.

Unusually for Turpin, he attempted no escape, even when being transported to the magistrate's court at Beverley under the watchful eye of just one local constable, Carey Gill. It would seem that he was content to take his punishment, but failed to realise that the proceedings that lay before him were far more serious than the investigation into the death of a gamecock.

Questions had been raised as to the source of his income and, having questioned Turpin (or Palmer) about his previous place of residence, the magistrates had contacted their counterparts at Long Sutton, Lincolnshire (where Turpin had previously attempted to lie low) who confirmed that Palmer had briefly lived in the town but had not been seen for a number of weeks. It was also revealed that the mysterious John Palmer was a wanted man, suspected of stealing livestock during his time in Lincolnshire, and had absconded from the custody of the local constable. As the theft of livestock was punishable by death, things had taken a very serious turn for the world-weary Dick Turpin.

The magistrate granted more time for the local constables to investigate the case and Turpin was removed to the more secure facilities of York Castle. It was during this brief stay that he would make the final, and most costly, error of his long and infamous career.

No doubt feeling melancholy and more than a little sorry for himself whilst caged in York Castle, Turpin decided to make contact with his family and penned a letter to his brother in law, Mr Rivernall (rumoured to be the only other member of the family who could read), telling him of his current situation, and how he came to be in such a predicament.

Unfortunately, upon receiving the letter, Rivernall remonstrated that he would not pay the postage, as he had no acquaintances in York; the letter was returned to the local post office, where one of Turpin's former schoolmasters instantly recognised the handwriting, and alerted the local magistrate. When opened, the letter left no doubt that John Palmer was Dick Turpin, and the schoolmaster, accompanied by the magistrate travelled to York over the following days where they would eventually provide a positive identification of the most wanted man in England, and claim a £200 reward between them (around £15,000 each in today's money).

The trial that followed was something of a showcase in that Turpin had no defence to the charges brought against him, especially the murder of Thomas Morris, yet hundreds of people packed the courtroom in order to catch a glimpse of the famous highwayman. This was very much an open and shut case, yet was drawn out over three days, possibly to allow as many people as possible to attend.

At the climax of the trial, the jury did not even need to leave the courtroom before delivering their verdict: Turpin was guilty as charged. Addressing the prisoner, the judge, Sir William Chapple, said 'your country has found you guilty of a crime worthy of death, it is my office to pronounce sentence upon you.'

If anything, Turpin seemed to take the news surprisingly well, and spent the next few days waiting for his execution whilst receiving a large number of visitors who treated him to ale and wine whilst catching up on old times. The gaoler is even rumoured to have made up to £100 from the sale of refreshments to Turpin and his constant entourage.

When the day of reckoning arrived, Turpin showed no fear as he was driven through the streets of York upon a cart, along with horse-thief John Stead. He even bowed to the crowds who lined the streets before reaching the gallows at Knavesmire. Climbing the steps to his oncoming death, Turpin shared a few words with the hangman who was, ironically, a convicted highwayman (York did not employ an executioner, the job was offered to convicted criminals in return for a reprieve). The manner of execution was a short drop, which would often result in the convict choking to death over a length of time, rather than being killed instantly as in the case of the long drop that would eventually replace this method of execution.

As the noose was placed around his head, Turpin did not wait for the hangman to assist him in stepping from the frame of the gallows; he went to his death on his own terms, taking a mighty leap before the rope tightened around his neck. It took just a few moments for Turpin to die. The corpse was allowed to hang for an hour before being taken to a local tavern where it was exhibited to the public for the entire evening. The next morning, the body was buried in the graveyard of St George's Church, Fishergate; and so ended the life of one of Britain's most infamous criminals. However, the incredible tale of Dick Turpin does not end here. His earthly remains were to stay in the ground for only a few days before local constables arrived at the graveyard one morning to be greeted with a grave in disarray and an empty coffin.

At this time, the York authorities were said to have turned a blind eye to body snatching, as most of the cadavers that went missing were put to use in the local medical school, for which the culprit would be handsomely rewarded, and with no family in York to object, it would seem that the matter was largely ignored by the police and magistrates. Given its central location, the churchyard was very much a public place, and so one can only surmise that not many people would have blinked an eyelid to the nocturnal digging, so common was this distasteful practice in the eighteenth century.

This macabre occurrence also split the conscience of the York townsfolk, as many of them saw Turpin as a celebrity and were keen to pay good money for any keepsake relating to the famous highwayman, whereas others, fearing the wrath of God, objected to this vile desecration, vowing to catch those responsible. A mob was formed, and the body snatchers were hunted throughout the city by those of a more religious persuasion. It did not take long to find them as, rather than being transported to the medical school, the body was being exhibited by a group of resurrection men, who were making a tidy profit from their illicit and impromptu exhibition. A melee ensued, during which the body was recovered and returned to the Church of St George for safekeeping, where it was eventually reburied – this time with quicklime covering the coffin, making any future attempts at resurrecting the highwayman impossible.

The man had been executed, resurrected, and reinterred, but his story would live on in the legend of his life. Although famed more for his criminal career than his posthumous appearance, the resurrection of Dick Turpin will always be one of the most famous examples of body snatching on record.

Part 2 – The Grateful Dead

We now travel back in time even further, arriving in the seventeenth century. The year may have changed, and the nature of the story, yet the location has not; we still find ourselves within the majestic spires and narrow winding alleyways of York.

As one would expect, this particular story does involve the exhumation of a coffin, and the removal of the inhabitant. However, everything else in this strange tale is unique. It is unlikely that the extraordinary events that took place in 1634 will ever be rivalled for the sheer surprise of what became of an unusual prisoner after his routine execution.

Nobody knows why John Bartendale was sentenced to hang. Every book or article in which he is mentioned states that he had been brought before the Assizes in York 'for some felony', an omission which is unfortunate, as often the crime for which a prisoner stands accused is helpful as a moral barometer in order to hazard a guess at the character of the man or woman in the dock.

However, this being 1634, there were an astonishing number of felonies for which Bartendale could have received a death sentence, many of which would be trivial misdemeanours in today's world, and others which would not be a crime at all! Having looked into some of the 220 crimes which were punishable by death, it is safe to say that many of them are laughable by today's standards, yet were taken extremely seriously in the seventeenth century, so that a person could be taken to the gallows for the most innocuous reasons.

One of the most bizarre 'crimes' to merit the death sentence was 'being in the company of Gypsies for one month or more', which would indicate that a couple of weeks in the company of Gypsies was absolutely fine, but one must be very careful not to step over that four week boundary! Another strange entry on the capital crimes list was 'strong evidence of malice in a child aged 7-14 years of age', which really does make one shudder. What on earth kind of malice could a child exhibit to be deemed suitable for execution?

Some of these examples were no doubt created in response to a crime which had actually been committed, which makes one wonder how gullible the militia must have been to fall for 'blacking the face whilst committing a crime'.

However, the carrying out of these punishments was, thankfully, a rare occurrence, with most executions being reserved for murder, rape, theft, and treason. Therefore, it is highly likely that our Mr Bartendale was not the kind of man who would be a welcome companion in a dark alley.

One thing we do know for sure about John Bartendale was that he was a travelling minstrel and piper, an occupation that has sadly been lost to the ravages of time, but was no doubt a legitimate career during the seventeenth century. He also had failed to take his sentence particularly seriously. Whatever the situation, Bartendale had found himself on the wrong end of the law, and was to spend his final days languishing in the condemned cell of York Castle, the very same facility that would later play host to Dick Turpin in his final days.

The minstrel was scheduled to end his life of travel and music on 27 March, and it has been rumoured that during this time, Bartendale was still a little unsure as to whether his execution would actually take place, believing that some divine intervention would save his life. Unfortunately for him, his execution did take place, and was held at the famous Micklegate Bar, later to be known as Knavesmire, which at this time was nothing more than an area of woodland situated at the perimeter of the city walls and far from the busy arena of execution which would appear over the next century along with the growth of the city.

The execution seemed to be performed flawlessly, with Bartendale putting up no fight whatsoever as he made his way to the scaffold. He faced his death like a true warrior, but this could also be explained by the fact that he still believed that somebody would come to his rescue.

However, nobody did, and just moments after his stoic arrival before the gallows, Bartendale found himself balancing upon a beam on the scaffold, waiting for his final moment to arrive. As Dick Turpin was to do in the next century, the piper stepped from the beam with no assistance, and his musical talent was lost forever.

As the drop was short, the officials stood by uncomfortably as their prisoner spent the next five minutes choking at the end of the rope, before finally falling silent. He was a powerful man and, as in so many cases, instinct had taken over as soon as he found himself hanging, and he fought with all his might to preserve the tiny spark of life that was left inside him. Owing to his strength, and the almighty fight he had put up against an unbeatable foe, the officials left the body of Bartendale hanging for three quarters of an hour, rather longer than they would have allowed for the average prisoner. The corpse was then cut down, and the executioner dismissed.

As Mickelgate Bar was still a rural area in the seventeenth century, the bodies of the executed criminals were buried in a copse not far from the scaffold. This allowed the burial to be concluded quickly and cheaply, and also ensured that the condemned would be laid to rest amongst people of their own ilk, rather than 'polluting' the graveyards of the righteous and holy.

As the last ounce of soil was placed upon the cheap and flimsy pauper's casket, the officials retreated to the castle, no doubt failing to give even a second thought to the body whose interment they had witnessed. Executions were ten a penny in that day and age, and very little care was taken of the body from the moment that life had been officially pronounced extinct.

The gravediggers had not done a particularly good job. They had dug down as far as they thought suitable, and then unceremoniously dumped the coffin into the hole, which was a great deal shallower than it should have been. However, all parties were keen to get out of the chilly March weather, and the lack of effort was universally ignored.

John Bartendale was now supposedly a lifeless corpse under a few feet of soil. Little did anyone know that this humble travelling piper was about to become a celebrity throughout the entire county, and that his execution would spawn a story so unlikely that it could be rivalled only by the epic tales of the Old Testament.

It was ironic that the first person to take a stroll through the wooded copse in which the Roman Catholic John Bartendale was buried, was one of the leading Catholics of the British gentry, who received a rather unexpected shock whilst enjoying his afternoon wandering through York's lush and verdant outskirts. Thomas Vavasour was better known as the Baronet of Haselwood, a castle inhabited by the Vavasours since the creation of the Domesday Book; the family would continue to inhabit the castle until the early twentieth century. Needless to say, the Baronet could wander wherever he pleased, and was not used to being disturbed.

Despite generations of the family enduring prejudice, and actual physical threat, during their long history, it must be assumed that what was about to happen to Thomas Vavasour was probably the most unusual incident ever to make it into the family memoirs. Enjoying the silence, and listening out for the distant birdsong, Vavasour soon became aware of an unexpected noise emanating from the copse. He stopped to make sense of the strange sound and, as he did so, he ordered his servant to halt and also to bring their horses (both of which the servant was leading) to a standstill.

The sound continued – faint, but audible to both men. It was some kind of strange scraping, which was interjected by sporadic banging – definitely not the kind of noise one would expect to hear whilst walking through a usually tranquil part of the Yorkshire countryside. No doubt suspecting an injured animal, or even suspicious goings on within the unmarked graveyard of the condemned prisoners, Vavasour and his servant slowly moved towards the source of the unusual noise, noting that it grew louder and more urgent the closer they approached.

It was at that point that the Baron noticed the ground begin to shake under their feet, the earth moving in time with the bangs, which originated from some subterranean source. Both men knew exactly what the purpose of this copse was and wondered to themselves whether this could really be what they were suspecting? With more than a little trepidation, the servant began to dig with his hands, and was soon joined by his master, who was clearly the type of gentleman who did not mind getting his hands dirty in the spirit of adventure, and would not stand idly whilst a servant toiled in his presence.

It did not take them long to reach the source of the commotion – a common wooden box which had been buried in the ground no more than 3ft below the surface. This was certainly a strange sight indeed, and with daggers drawn and much caution, they cleared the remaining debris from the casket and lifted the lid. The sight that greeted them was nothing short of terrifying; a naked man, filthy and rambling incoherently sprang from the box like some grotesque Jack-in-the-Box. Both men fell to the ground in shock, taking a few moments to realise what they had just witnessed, and trying to make sense of this bizarre occurrence. As the Baron regained his composure, he ordered the servant to help this mysterious creature from the box and, lending a hand, manoeuvred the frantic stranger to the graveside, where he was then seated and covered with the cloak of the inquisitive nobleman.

The mud-caked apparition was feverishly asking questions. 'Where am I?' 'How did I get here?' and most tellingly, 'Am I in Heaven?' Apart from the question about Heaven, the Baron and his servant were unable to answer these queries, but both of them had their suspicions of whence the man had come. The servant was sent for water and food in order to provide sustenance for the wretched character, but before he had chance to return, several more people had wandered by the copse and were now surrounding the muddy stranger, keen to catch a glimpse of the man who had been so theatrically resurrected. Crowds began to gather as the word spread and, before long, the copse was awash with people, all of whom had arrived to congratulate Bartendale on his miraculous feat. In this age of religious piety, the sight of a resurrected man was something which none of the open-mouthed onlookers would ever forget. Sadly, the commotion was heard of by the officials of York Castle, who immediately sent out a party to investigate. One can only surmise that there were a few red faces within the castle walls when Bartendale was escorted back to his previous abode, as alive as he had been when he was taken from his cell that very same morning.

It has been reported that Thomas Vavasour was inconsolable that the resurrected piper had been returned to prison, as he later stated that, had the crowd not appeared, he would have removed the man to his own estate and conveyed him to another part of the country in order to live out the life he had been given for a second time.

However, a question now arose as to what to do with John Bartendale. Some argued that the sentence imposed on him had been to be 'hanged by the neck until dead', and reasoned that the travelling minstrel should be taken back to the scaffold and subjected to another execution. Yet others argued that Bartendale had received his punishment, and that his miraculous survival was nothing more than an act of God, something with which, thankfully, the judge who had originally sentenced Bartendale agreed. It would have been almost sacrilegious to execute a man who appeared to have been saved by the hand of the Almighty, and so the man who survived his own execution was brought before the court once more, and given a full and free pardon for his crimes.

There have been a few theories as to how Bartendale survived his execution, the most common being that, having been a piper for many years, the musician had developed a strong windpipe and an extraordinary lung capacity during his long career. Another theory is that Bartendale struggled so mightily whilst hanging that he managed to somehow loosen the rope before falling unconscious, and was mistakenly assumed to be dead, although this theory does rely very much on coincidence, especially as his body was left to hang for forty-five minutes.

Yet, if there is anything that the tale of the resurrected piper is not short of, it is coincidence. For a man to survive being hanged, and then to be discovered whilst hammering at the inside of his coffin in a rural woodland where footfall was fairly scarce, is nothing short of incredible.

Another theory, which has only been sporadically suggested yet seems to be the most believable of all, is that Bartendale had cheated the hangman by inserting a small length of metal pipe into his throat, thus preventing his windpipe from being crushed. This would have been especially successful in this kind of hanging, as a short drop would also render the chance of a broken neck extremely unlikely. It would also explain the lack of fear shown by Bartendale in the days and hours before he was to be executed. It does not, however, explain the extraordinary luck he experienced in managing to alert a passer-by, especially one who treated the prisoner with so much care and concern. Some have suggested that the whole thing was a ruse, with Vavasour being complicit in saving the life of a fellow Catholic; no other link between the two men has ever been established, however.

Whatever the reason for this spectacular resurrection, Baretendale had cheated death, and was now a free man. With no further reason to stay in York, and being able to live on his improbable story for a good while, the minstrel began to travel once more, but was eventually to settle down as an inn-keeper somewhere in North Yorkshire. One would imagine that Bartendale was a popular inn-keeper, and was very likely to have been the recipient of many an admiring comment and flagon of ale. After all, where else could you drink in the company of a man who had died and been buried?

Even by the time he had reached old age, his customers and friends had not tired of hearing the tale of the resurrected piper from the man himself, and his story was even immortalised in a popular song which was, no doubt a regular ditty in the hostelry of John Bartendale, the man who had cheated death, and possibly the law.

> *Here a piper apprehended,*
> *Was found guilty and suspended,*
> *Being led to fatal gallows,*
> *Boys did cry 'Where is thy bellows?'*
> *Ever must though cease thy turning,*
> *Aswered he for all thy cunning,*
> *You may fail in your prediction.*
> *Which did happen without fiction*
> *For cut down and quick interred,*
> *Earth rejected which was buried,*
> *Half alive and dead he rises,*
> *Got a pardon next assizes,*
> *And in York continued blowing-*
> *Yet a sense of goodness showing.*

Whatever your opinion of this strange tale, it is unique in the dark realm of body-snatching folklore, as Bartendale could well be the only man who was ever dragged from his grave in an act of kindness, and definitely the only corpse to have gone on to lead a full and happy life! While much of the tale is based on conjecture, mainly due to the age of the reports, it does remain a popular anecdotal story in and around North Yorkshire, but has sadly been allowed to slip from the pages of national folklore, save for a few compendiums of bizarre facts and gruesome stories.

Yet, this lurid story of resurrection deserves to be preserved, if only as a shining example of the ease in which death sentences were handed out, and the lackadaisical attitude often taken by officials during the execution of the condemned prisoners. It is also an important source in tracking the evolution of both execution and burial over the centuries. Even by the time that the infamous Dick Turpin swung from the gallows on the very same spot, much had changed in both the city and the attitude to taking the lives of condemned convicts.

As for the future of the Knavesmire gallows, they went on to be the venue for many public executions over the next two centuries, and became part of the greater outreaches of York by the early eighteenth century. Thousands of souls would have breathed their last upon this historic ground, and the outskirts of the city would have been the last thing any of them ever saw.

By the beginning of the nineteenth century however, it had been decided that the site of the gallows, and the often raucous public executions, were perhaps not the best way to greet visitors to the city, as the area was now used as a main thoroughfare to the historic city centre.

The gallows were moved to a more discreet venue in 1801, where public executions could still take place, but were largely hidden by the mighty walls of the castle; altogether a more tasteful solution, if one could ever describe public executions as tasteful.

The Knavesmire is now largely used for leisure purposes, with part of the old woodland now making up the far boundaries of the famous York Racecourse, and the other part being used as a public park, popular for dog walking, picnicking, and public events.

Yet, one wonders how many of the people who frequently use the park are aware of its macabre past, and have any knowledge as to the earthly remains of the convicts that lie beneath. It is certainly possible that a number of Yorkshire folk could have picnicked on the spot where John Bartendale rose from the dead all those years ago.

Chapter 1

The Birth of the Resurrectionists

'In selfish men, caution is as secure an armour for their foes as for themselves.'

Bram Stoker – Dracula

Part 1 – A Map of Progress

During the late eighteenth and early nineteenth century, the developed world had changed almost beyond recognition from that of earlier periods in history. One of the main priorities in many societies was education, which was, at that time, rivalling religion as the yardstick of the civilised world.

Especially important in this new inquisitive age were both scientific and medical research, and to begin the great journey into the unknown, the obvious starting point was one very close to home: the intimate workings of the wondrous human body. To make the mapping and identification of each area of the human body possible, the only method of research was by means of dissection, something which had been viewed as ungodly and immoral in the past, and would continue to be judged with horror and mistrust for many generations to come.

Dissection had been used before, notably by the Italian renaissance intellectuals and ground-breaking thinkers, such as Leonardo da Vinci, who would be long deceased before the genius of his prolific work became apparent to the educated world. Human dissection went back much further than this however, having been studied in both India and Tibet – where the Buddhist religion would often employ a 'sky burial' to dispose of their dead. This involved a ritual dissection, after which certain parts of the body were fed to the vultures that inhabited the mountain tops. This was more from necessity than anything else, as, especially in Tibet, the ground was often frozen and burial was not an option. There was also a distinct shortage of wood, which would have been necessary for cremation.

Europe was a little slower in delving into the workings of the human body, largely due to religious decrees that had been followed to the letter, but were often ambiguous in their message, leading to the god-fearing folk of the Dark Ages perceiving such an act to be a direct affront on their creator. By the fourteenth century however, the Italians, as was so often the case, recognised the importance of dissection in medical research, and a law was passed that every doctor must attend a dissection at some point during their career. Unfortunately, these dissections would be organised by the State, and would take place only once every five years! Yet the laws began to relax almost immediately, and it was in 1315 that Modino de Luzzi, a physician, anatomist and surgeon, performed the first recorded dissection, of which the documents produced can still be seen in specialist museums today. The procedure was carried out in public, and was well attended by scholars and other men of learning. Three men were tasked with the duty: de Luzzi, who would act as the Lector (who conducted the lecture during the dissection), a Sector (who would actually perform the dissection), and an Ostensor, (an assistant given the duty of pointing out areas of interest to the assembled spectators). It would be ninety-one years before this procedure would be performed outside of Italy, but the dissection was performed by an Italian surgeon, Glaeazzo di Santa Sofia, who travelled north to Vienna in 1404 to showcase the methods of human dissection. Despite their reticence in accepting the benefits of dissection, the Catholic Church did order an autopsy in 1533, in which the bodies of conjoined twins, Joana and Melchiora Ballestero were examined in order to determine whether the two sisters shared a soul! (It was decided that they didn't, as they each possessed their own heart, which the church at that time accepted to be the source of the soul).

As time went on, the seat of medical progress eventually shifted from Italy to Britain, although the British were very slow in catching up with their European cousins in terms of anatomy, as dissection remained entirely forbidden until the sixteenth century, when a series of royal edicts gave permission to certain individuals in very specific circumstances.

Even by the mid-eighteenth century, the societies of both surgeons and physicians were only allowed ten corpses between them each year. This resulted in a fierce fight for a place in the lecture theatre, with audiences in their thousands being reported at certain lectures which, legend has it, caused a number of ugly scenes. Rapidly, the number of medical schools around the country began to increase, and by the mid eighteenth century, the corpses allotted to these establishments were insufficient to say the least. Reminding the government of Britain's current lead in the race for knowledge, the anatomists began to put pressure on the leaders of the nation. This resulted in the 1752 Murder Act, in which it was stated that the body of any convict executed for murder would be made available to the anatomists, therefore aiding the flourishing medical schools, and giving the convicts a chance to prove themselves useful to society after death (not that they were given any choice in the matter).

Yet, just a hundred years later, this arrangement was found to be inadequate, as the rise in medical study had resulted in most large towns and cities boasting its own School of Medicine and Anatomy, all of which required a steady supply of fresh cadavers. There were simply not enough corpses to go around, and as these were only granted to the public medical schools, and forbidden to private schools, something had to change in order to keep medical establishments from closing their doors to students.

It was not the government who would eventually relent and provide extra bodies to the schools, it was the rise of a black market commodity, which was seized upon by many disreputable (and some previously reputable) individuals who would create the flourishing industry on which this book is based. The schools had no choice but to turn a blind eye to the source of their expensively obtained specimens, and as such, the medical profession now straddled the boundaries of the legitimate world of education, and the illegal world of the wealth-seeking resurrection men. This grey area would also see a blind eye being turned by the law, especially as the ruling classes were largely aware of the current situation, and recommended surprisingly lenient sentences for any individual who had steadily lowered themselves into the murky waters of the body trade. As a result, the resurrectionists were now out in force and, in many cases, this questionable profession became the main source of income for families the length and breadth of the nation. A large sum could be commanded for a fresh corpse, and many such families would go on to lead very comfortable lives during the rise of the body snatchers.

Part 2 – North of the Border

In order to set the scene for the events which highlight the risks and rewards as life as a resurrection man, it is necessary to leave Yorkshire for a short while, and set our sights upon the centre of the body snatching trade, which, as many will be aware, was the Scottish metropolis, and capital city, of Edinburgh. Many will also be aware of the story that follows, as it remains, even today, the most famous of the body snatching stories, and serves as the perfect example of a situation where a small fortune could be made quickly and easily from the misfortune of others. This is not to say that other cities, namely York, Leeds and Sheffield, did not find themselves in the grip of the resurrectionist trade, these crimes were almost as prevalent in these areas as they were in Edinburgh; yet the Scottish capital is where many of the bodies ended up, and is also where two such criminals took things one step further in pursuit of wealth.

It becomes necessary at this point to introduce two men of Irish birth, who, for one reason or another, found themselves in Edinburgh, the epicentre of the resurrectionist movement. No study of body snatching written anywhere in the world can be produced without the mention of the infamous and shocking tale of Burke and Hare. These two men personify the evils of body snatching like no others, and would adapt the unique situation of the medical schools to their own advantage.

William Burke was born in Ulster in 1792, and after trying, and failing, to make a living in a number of professions, decide to leave his wife and children in poverty and move to Scotland, from where he promised he would send money, but eventually lost all contact with the people who depended upon him the most. Finding work on the creation of the Union Canal, Burke soon forgot all about his loving wife, and found himself a mistress, Helen McDougal, who would, from this day forward, follow her lover into a world of moral darkness and illegally obtained riches. Whilst working on the Union Canal, Burke became acquainted with another navvy, a fellow Irishman by the name of William Hare, of whom the *Newry Telegraph* provided a detailed description in an article published 31 March 1829, which paints the future criminal in quite a terrifying light.

Hare was born and bred about one half mile distant from Scarva in the opposite county of Armagh and shortly before his departure from this country he lived in the service of Mr Hall, the keeper of the eleventh lock near Poyntzpass. He was chiefly engaged in driving the horses which his master employed in hauling lighters on the Newry Canal.

He was always remarkable for being of a ferocious and malignant disposition, an instance of which he gave in the killing of one of his Master's horses, which obliged him to flee to Scotland where he perpetrated those unparalleled crimes that must always secure him a conspicuous page in the annals of murder.

This new friendship bore a mutual benefit because Hare and his wife, Margaret, ran a small boarding house in the West Port area of the city, and Burke, and the woman publically posing as his wife, were in need of cheap lodgings. From hereon in, the two men became inseparable, both at work and at home. Even blessed with a firm friendship, life in the West Port district was hard, and the two couples fought a daily battle to survive on the meagre wages paid by the construction company. Until, that is, an unfortunate event provided the chance of an unexpected, yet welcome, windfall.

One of the other lodgers in Hare's property was a retired soldier by the name of Donald Bark, who died of natural causes one night, leaving Burke and Hare with the unenviable task of ridding themselves of an unclaimed body, and also leaving Hare out of pocket to the tune of £4, which the deceased had owed in rent for the small room he inhabited alone. As they pondered their situation, the two men soon hit upon a brainwave; both problems could be solved in one fell swoop. It was constant talk on the streets of Edinburgh that the medical schools were always in need of corpses, and here was one, who just happened to have died whilst in debt to a ruthless and opportunistic man.

Bark was placed into a cheaply bought coffin, which was then sealed and sent to an undertaker to dispose of in the traditional manner of a funeral. This being very much a pauper's funeral, the 'body' was never removed from the cheap coffin, and was buried with very few witnesses, and no questions asked. The body was then taken in a sack through the streets of Edinburgh, where a large bundle on a cart would have drawn no attention, given the sheer amount of construction work being undertaken in and around the city at that time. Upon arriving in the vicinity of the medical schools, the two men, according to later testimony, asked for directions to the well known Dr Munro, but guessing correctly at what was in the sack, the medical student who had been asked for assistance directed the two man and their cargo in the direction of Surgeon's Square, and to the offices of Dr Robert Knox.

Knox was a well-known surgeon in medical circles, having first gained his extensive knowledge of anatomy during the Battle of Waterloo, where he had served as an army surgeon with an excellent reputation. He then went on to become a revered anatomist, and a man upon whom many would rely for a high standard of teaching, and a veritable wealth of knowledge.

An assistant at the medical school had no hesitation in paying over £7 for the corpse, almost double the amount which was owed to Hare, an amount of money which would put food on the boarding house table for the next few months, and also provide the men with welcome funds to spend every evening in the local inns and taverns. It was during one of these evenings that Burke and Hare reflected on their recent good fortune, and decided upon a plan which was as illegal as it was horrific, but would see the two couples living in relative luxury for the foreseeable future. More money could be obtained with more bodies, but as there were no more corpses in their possession, they soon realised that one way around this obstacle was to simply 'create' bodies, which could then be sold for exorbitant sums to their new and reputable investor.

In the space of less than a week, a second business opportunity was identified. Another tenant of Hare's, an elderly man named Joseph, had fallen gravely ill. After the opportunist pair had given their housemate time to die naturally however, it was decided that maybe steps should be taken to hurry things along. This was the moment where the pair's signature method of murder was invented. They would smother the victim until dead, being careful to leave no marks, in order to prevent any detectable injuries being present when the body was examined by the anatomists. Although the step up from merely selling a corpse to creating one was something of a departure, in both practicality and morality, Burke and Hare were successful in carrying out their plans, albeit slightly squeamishly and amateurishly on their first attempt.

Again, the school of Dr Knox paid a handsome sum for the cadaver and no questions whatsoever were asked as to the cause of death, or method of obtaining the body. This was easy money, but the escalation from petty profiteering to murder was one that both men knew could one day lead to unthinkable consequences. Extra care had been taken due to the more serious nature of the crime being committed, and the transportation of the body was done by the use of an old tea chest, rather than a large sack. This, the men reasoned, provided extra security because the box could be locked whilst in transit.

With their own safety aforethought, Burke and Hare bided their time before selecting a second victim, and lived on the proceeds of the two previous transactions for as long as possible, although the frivolous spending of the illicit money did mean that the proceeds of crime did not last as long as planned. With funds running low, Abigail Simpson, who had been in Edinburgh for the market and could not find any passage home, was invited to spend a night at the lodging house, and after plying their unfortunate victim, the two murderous resurrectionists set about smothering the life from their house guest. Utilising the tea chest, they arranged to meet a porter from Dr Knox's school the next morning, and lifted their criminally obtained goods onto a waiting cart, on which it was transported to the anatomy tables. This time, due to the healthy corpse, and the fact that the deceased was younger than the previous two offerings, the fee had gone up to £10, which was gladly paid by the porter on behalf of his employer.

As time went on, this vile venture became more of a family business than a secret hobby, as both Margaret Hare and Helen McDougal became complicit in the activities of their respective partners. In fact, by the time the two killers had plotted their next crime, the fearsome Mrs Hare was a critical part of the tawdry operation.

The next victim was enticed to the house by Mrs Hare, but what kind of enticement was offered has never been documented. The unwary guest was then plied with the usual strong alcohol before William Hare arrived back at the house and took over from his wife in carrying out the most unpleasant part of the procedure. Burke had been given an opportunity to sit this one out, but the next victim was dealt with by Burke himself, without the need for an accomplice. As all proceeds of the crime were shared equally between the couples, it would seem that this lucrative business also incorporated shift work!

Business went from strength to strength and, as the pockets of Burke and Hare became fuller, the population of Edinburgh reduced. All in all, sixteen corpses were dispatched to the medical schools by the two Irishmen, and only one of these was dead before they came into the possession of the wily body traders. There were a couple of bumps along the way; one such problem being raised after the murder of a well-known young man from the local area. James Wilson, known as 'Daft Jamie', was something of a character around West Port, and when his body appeared on the slab the day after his mysterious death, several of the medical students recognised the eccentric young man. Dr Knox, who was well aware of the identity of his supplier, denied that the body was that of Wilson. The students, however, found it strange that this particular body was chosen to be dissected before the others in the possession of the school, and even stranger was the fact that, by the time the body was prepared for dissection, the head had been entirely removed.

The sixteenth and final cadaver was also to cause serious issues for Burke and Hare because the victim, middle-aged Irishwoman, Mary Docherty, put up quite a struggle, and the commotion was overheard by James and Ann Gray, another couple who rented a room from William Hare and his wife. The commotion was so loud that the couple left the house for the night and returned only the next morning, after informing friends that they had heard a great deal of banging and shouting. Mrs Gray also claimed that she heard a woman's voice shouting 'murder!' before they left the house to seek tranquillity elsewhere.

This was to be the mistake that would end the Burke and Hare resurrection business, and would also result in dire consequences for those involved. All it took was a middle-aged woman of sufficient strength to put up a fight against the two burly Irishmen, and the whole enterprise came crashing down around the ears of the two criminal couples.

Part 3 – Infamy and Consequence

Blissfully unaware that their fellow residents had been party to the noises of the previous night, Mr and Mrs Hare chose this particular murder to let their guard drop. It would be this lack of care and attention that would see the group relieved of any further income, and also set to face far more serious consequences. The Grays returned early the following morning to find their landlady acting particularly strangely. The couple were advised not to go into one particular room, and were told in no uncertain terms not to go near the bed in that room under any circumstances. Intrigued by this unusual warning, the couple immediately took the chance to inspect the room as soon as Mrs Hare had left the house to go to the market. In doing so, they soon discovered the body of Mary Docherty, and fled the house to alert the police.

Whilst hurrying to the police station, the Grays ran into Helen McDougal, who casually offered them a retainer of £10 per week if they were to change their minds about involving the police. The couple refused, pushed their way past McDougal, and continued their mad dash in the direction of the police station. McDougal had obviously arrived home quickly, because by the time the police arrived the body was nowhere to be seen. However, when questioned separately, McDougal claimed that Mrs Docherty had left the previous evening, and Burke claimed that she had stayed until that morning. Faced with this telling difference in the story, the police immediately arrested Burke and his mistress, and lay in wait for the Hares upon their return.

Meanwhile, an anonymous tip off had been received, which led the police to the dissection room of Dr Knox, in which they found the body of Mary Docherty, which was positively identified by James Gray. By that evening, all four members of the resurrection gang had been rounded up and placed into police custody. By the time the case came to trial, it was apparent to anyone with legal training that the evidence against all four parties was insufficient for the case to continue. No visible cause of death could be established in Mary Docherty, whose body was the only real piece of evidence available to the courts. Refusing to be beaten, the judge then adjourned the proceedings, before approaching Hare and offering him the once in a lifetime chance of turning King's evidence. If Burke could be tried for the murder, then Hare would walk free from court. It was a tough decision, but self-preservation won through in the end, and Hare prepared to double-cross his partner in crime.

By the time the case reopened, the four defendants in the dock had been reduced to just two, with Mrs Hare being adjudged to have acted under the direction of her husband, who was known to be a frightening and violent individual (although many testimonies would suggest that Mrs Hare was every bit as frightening as her husband!).

Yet, most would testify that Hare was the more barbaric of the two men and should have been the one facing execution for the crimes. However, the trial went ahead, and the scenes in the courtroom on that day, Christmas Eve of 1828, was described in great detail by a journalist working for a the Illustrated Edinburgh News

> *By orders from the Court a large window was thrown open as far as it could be done, and a current of cold damp air beat for twenty-four hours upon the heads of the whole audience. The greater part of the audience being Advocates and Writers to the Signet in their gowns, these were wrapped round their heads, and, intermingled with various coloured handkerchiefs in every shade and form of drapery, which gave to the visages that were enshrouded under them such a grim and grisly aspect as assimilated them to a college of monks or inquisitors, or characters imagined in tales of romance, grouped and contrasted most fantastically with the costume of the bench and the crowded bar engaged in the trial.*

For a full twenty-four hours the court examined all evidence available, and heard a number of testimonies which supported the charges against Burke and McDougal (Helen McDougal had not been acquitted, possibly due to her having acted independently in offering money to Mr and Mrs Gray), and by the time the decision of the jury had been reached, it would be Christmas Day, yet no presents would be under the tree for William Burke this year. The jury retired for fifty minutes, and when they emerged, the foreman revealed that the twelve good men had found Burke guilty of the murder of Mary Docherty, and gave their opinion that he was guilty of many, many more acts of abhorrent evil. On sentencing William Burke to death, the judge, Lord Justice-Clerk David Boyle, also made a decision that would please the spectators in court, and add a little more Christmas cheer to the good folk of Edinburgh. Burke was not only to hang, his body was also to be dissected on the very slabs that his victims had lain upon just weeks earlier.

You now stand convicted, by the verdict of a most respectable jury of your country, of the atrocious murder charged against you in this indictment, upon evidence which carried conviction to the mind of every man that heard it.

In regard to your case, the only doubt that has come across my mind is, whether, in order to mark the sense that the Court entertains of your offence, and which the violated laws of the country entertain respecting it, your body should not be exhibited in chains, in order to deter others from the like crimes in time coming.

But, taking into consideration that the public eye would be offended with so dismal an exhibition, I am disposed to agree that your sentence shall be put in execution in the usual way, but accompanied with the statutory attendant of the punishment of the crime of murder, that your body should be publicly dissected and anatomized.

And I trust, that if it is ever customary to preserve skeletons, yours will be preserved, in order that posterity may keep in remembrance of your atrocious crimes.

The execution took place just over a month later, and William Burke (McDougal had been released, but had been hounded from the city by baying mobs) was hanged at 8.15am on 28 January in front of a crowd that numbered between twenty and thirty thousand people.

His body was then immediately taken to the Anatomy Theatre of Edinburgh University, where it was prepared for dissection by Professor Alexander Munro, the man who had been the intended recipient for the very first body to be sold by Burke and Hare. The dissection was delayed by a number of hours due to near rioting caused by the limited number of tickets granted for this particular lecture. Order was finally restored when Munro agreed for the body to be laid out after the dissection, for inspection by those who did not have tickets. The procedure took two hours to complete, and the highlight of the lecture came when Professor Munro dipped his pen into the blood of the body snatcher, and wrote on a piece of parchment 'This is written with the blood of Wm Burke, who was hanged at Edinburgh. This blood was taken from his head.'

The whereabouts of the parchment is currently unknown, but other artefacts from the dissection are on exhibition in the Edinburgh Surgeon's Hall Museum, such as a book made from his tanned skin, and a death mask taken just before the dissection. His entire skeleton also hangs in the Anatomical Museum of the Edinburgh Medical School.

And as for the rest of the gang? Well, as mentioned above, Helen McDougal was chased from the city by a constant mob of angry citizens who followed her every move. Her safety was only achieved when she was smuggled through the rear door of a police station in men's clothing. She would eventually be seen heading for Durham, where all record of her ceased to exist. A similar fate lay in store for Mrs Hare, who was also targeted by the angry Edinburgh folk, and was chased from city to city until the police took mercy upon her, and placed her on a ferry to Belfast, where she would then make her way to her home county of Derry. Like McDougal, she was never heard of again.

Hare's release was equally eventful. He was placed on a mail coach heading for Dumfries, where he was recognised by somebody who had been involved in the court proceedings. As a result, news that Hare was in the town spread quicker than a forest fire, and Hare could only throw himself at the mercy of the Dumfries police, who placed him on another coach out of the town, from where he was driven south, and advised to cross the border into England and never to return to Scotland.

Two sightings were made of the cowardly killer on the outskirts of Carlisle around a month later, but no formal sighting was ever made after this. Although tales of Hare's comeuppance are commonly told, these are unsupported by any evidence – although they could easily be true, such was the hatred of the nation for this undeservedly free killer. The most popular legend is that Hare was thrown into a lime pit, which resulted in him being rendered blind for the rest of his life, which was spent as a beggar on the streets of London. However, as mentioned, there are no reliable sources to confirm this.

Dr Knox was cleared of all accusations in light of Hare confirming that the source of the cadavers was never revealed during their business transactions. His liberty may have been secured by this admission, but nothing could be done to repair his reputation, and the rest of his career was spent under the dark shadow of the West Port murders.

Part 4 – From the Ashes

As will be studied in detail towards the end of this compendium, the Burke and Hare case was one of the main catalysts behind a large-scale change in the governance of corpses used by the anatomy schools in the future, such was the public outcry to this case, and certain others which followed.

So ingrained in the public conscience were the West Port murders, that children even incorporated the tale into a rhyme, which would be recited innocently as went about their carefree lives. Something that would no doubt annoy the two brutal and heartless killers, who ended many lives for nothing more than their own personal gain.

> *Up the close and doun the stair,*
> *But and ben wi' Burke and Hare.*
> *Burke's the butcher, Hare's the thief,*
> *Knox the boy that buys the beef.*

The Anatomy Act which was to be passed through the House of Commons just two years after the execution of William Burke would change the face of medical research forever, and would also, ironically, ensure that Burke would be one of the very last convicts to be dissected after execution.

Just after the passing of the Anatomy Act, the medical journal, *The Lancet* published a very interesting piece, which linked the case of Burke and Hare to the eventual passing of the act, and their unwitting influence on the medical profession as a whole.

> *Burke and Hare, it is said, are the real authors of the measure, and that which would never have been sanctioned by the deliberate wisdom of parliament, is about to be extorted from its fears.*

It would have been well if this fear had been manifested and acted upon before sixteen human beings had fallen victims to the supineness of the Government and the Legislature.

It required no extraordinary sagacity, to foresee that the worst consequences must inevitably result from the system of traffic between resurrectionists and anatomists, which the executive government has so long suffered to exist.

Government is already in a great degree, responsible for the crime which it has fostered by its negligence, and even encouraged by a system of forbearance.

The sixteen victims referred to above are rarely mentioned in relation to the West Port murders, as the gaudy and thrill-seeking world of crime writing does not usually find the victims to be of much importance when retelling a tale which contains such shocking acts. The dead usually find themselves reduced to minor characters within the wider story. However, due to the detailed confessions of William Burke, one of which was made to the courts, and the other to the press, it was possible to compile a list of the victims and it seems only fitting, after giving so much time to their depraved killers, to end the chapter by publically reintroducing these poor victims to the world. Unfortunately the details for many of the victims are sparse, such was the lack of humanity shown by their killers, who certainly did not have any interest in the lives of these sixteen human beings, who proved to be nothing more than business commodities in the grand scheme of the Burke and Hare enterprise.

Donald Bark, army pensioner (not killed by Burke and Hare)
Abigail Simpson from Gilmerton, salt seller
Joseph, a millworker
Drunken female lodger (Killed by Burke alone)
English male lodger from Cheshire
Mary Haldane, prostitute
Effie, cinder-gatherer
Irish woman from Glasgow
Glasgow woman's son or grandson
Female lodger (Killed by Hare alone)
Drunken woman in the West Port

Mary Paterson, also known as Mary Mitchell
Mrs Hostler, washerwoman
Ann McDougal, from Falkirk (estranged cousin of Helen McDougal)
James Wilson, known as 'Daft Jamie'
Mary Docherty, Irish beggar woman; also known as Margery Campbell

Perhaps the most damning appraisal of the West Port murders can be found in a passage by Sir Walter Scott, in which his tongue in cheek comments criticise the lack of humanity shown by Burke and Hare, and also highlights just how cheap life could be in the inner cities of the nineteenth century.

Our Irish importation have made a great discovery of Economics, namely, that a wretch who is not worth a farthing while alive, becomes a valuable article when knocked on the head and carried to an anatomist; and acting on this principle, have cleared the streets of some of those miserable offcasts of society, whom nobody missed because nobody wished to see them again.

Chapter 2

Fanning the Flames

'The fire which seems extinguished often slumbers beneath the ashes.'
Pierre Corneille – Rodogune

Part 1 – A Man of the People

The successful business and social standing of Samuel Roberts had been hard-earned, his life devoted to working in the silver and metal plating business, a lifelong vocation which had been thrust upon him at the tender age of 14.

Having worked his way through every department and rank at his father's Sheffield factory by the age of 21, there reached a point where Roberts had nothing left to learn from his humble and hardworking patriarch; this led to a mutual parting of ways, but one in which neither party felt any malice. Taking with him a friend who had developed in the business along with Roberts, having started his apprenticeship at the same time, Roberts and his father agreed that the metalworking industry of Sheffield could easily support two family businesses, and so Samuel left to make his own way in the world.

Possessing an iron will and unrivalled business acumen, it was not long before he had this new factory and was enjoying a healthy share of the local industry, a fact that pleased father and son alike. Yet despite achieving such success at an early age, Roberts would not allow his new-found wealth to eclipse the energy and passion for life that had blossomed during his apprentice days. Nor would he allow his new social standing to mask the hard upbringing, which had prepared him for life as a successful manufacturer. He was a working-man from an early age, and would continue to identify with, and fight the cause of Sheffield's workers, albeit from a loftier position. It was this moral and social sense of responsibility that led Roberts to put pen to paper, and write a number of essays, which were gladly published by the local press. Before long, the written opinions of Samuel Roberts were in demand, and very rarely did a week go by without a contribution to the newspapers.

Despite this burgeoning literary career, Roberts made the decision at an early stage that he would never write for profit, and would only allow his work to be published if he firmly believed that it was favourable to the morality of the Sheffield public. Subjects routinely tackled by Roberts included slave labour, child labour, capital punishment and war, all of which were causes close to his heart, and which brought out the passion and sense of camaraderie instilled in him since his days as an apprentice boy. However, despite his obvious benevolence and intelligence, there was one literary offering which lit the touch paper to a chain of events so grievous, that it would damage the educational reputation of Sheffield for a long time, and would spark a shameful incident that would forever live on in the history of his native city.

It started with a fairly mundane and routine legal battle, in which Roberts had taken considerable issue with the tenancy of a building, which had been left to him by a recently deceased relative, and who had named Samuel as the sole executor of his estate. The rather grand building on Eyre Street had been recently taken over by the new and controversial Sheffield School of Anatomy, having been signed over by his late relative, and a contract drawn up to allow their school to use the premises. The first School of Anatomy had been situated in Church Street, but had proven too small for the requirements of the school, so new premises were required, and quickly obtained by the founding fathers of the institution.

Sheffield had actually been home to a Medical School for the last five years, but in addition to this, Dr Corden Thompson and Mr Wilson Overend petitioned for, and succeeded in adding, a separate School of Anatomy to the city's educational arsenal. Having originally been given the Church Street premises, the developments in the study of Anatomy, and the changing face of science in general had seen a marked increase in the number of applicants wishing to study within the city. It was for this very reason that the tenancy of the Eyre Street premises had been granted, as Roberts's relative had recognised a flourishing business, and in light of this, was able to ask for a considerable amount of rent in return for the use of his property.

But, as we know from his literary resolutions, Samuel Roberts was not a man who could easily forget his morality, or bury his feelings of mistrust. It was this feeling of distaste towards the goings-on in his newly acquired property which led Roberts to initiate court proceedings. It does seem rather naive that such a wise man would challenge the contents of a legally binding contract but, as the owner of the property, Roberts believed that he had the right to evict a tenant if he disagreed with practices being performed under his own roof.

The courts, and the directors of the school firmly disagreed however, leaving Roberts frustrated and defeated by the signed contract, which was waved under his nose during the proceedings. It was this sense of anger and hostility that led Roberts to hit back in the only way he saw fit. The thorny issue of human dissection had long been a talking point in every walk of society, and with this in mind, Roberts decided to pen a new essay on the evils of the Anatomists and the macabre practices which took place behind the closed doors of the building he owned. Whether through genuine concern, or as a clever way to elicit public support, Roberts used the essay (which he then also published as a pamphlet) to tackle the issue of dissection as a class issue, rather than one of morality and religious concern.

Ever since the practice of dissection (on those other than executed murderers) had been legalised by the Anatomy Act, the fear of being taken to the medical schools and being used as a learning device had caused considerable concern to the poor and weak. Something that, Roberts argued, would not be inflicted upon the rich and successful. He argued that dissection of convicted killers had only been allowed in certain cases, and was seen as a further punishment for those who had committed especially grievous acts of murder, stating that it was 'so horrible, that it was not decreed even amongst common murderers, but only against the most atrocious of them.' In possession of the full knowledge that workhouses, and the landlords of slum housing, could now sell the bodies of their deceased tenants to the Anatomy School, especially if rent was owing at the time of death, Roberts went on to challenge the practice:

Have the rich, then, any right to doom those who are compelled by poverty to demand relief, on that account, to any species of punishment? Certainly not; any more than the other members of a sick club have to inflict punishment on the sick members. But the rich have done this!

He went on to warn the public that the Anatomy Act, and the subsequent rise in the need for cadavers, would turn the medical schools into 'nothing more than Burking houses', using the famous case of Burke and Hare to further fan the flames of unrest.

The timing of the essay could not have been better for Roberts, as the issue was also sparking much debate in the House of Lords at the time, with several Lords, including the Earl of Harewood, giving their opinions both in the House, and also in the national press. The Earl himself had publically stated that he 'did not see why the bodies of the poor and friendless should be particularly selected for the dissecting knife'; a sentiment that echoed the very concerns which Roberts raised in his own publication.

The mood of the public, especially the poor and sick, was darkened by the opening of old wounds, and from this point onwards, the sturdy doors of the School of Anatomy were eyed with great suspicion and fear by those who had the courage to even walk past this building of ungodly practices. All it would take to stir the Sheffield residents into a frenzy of reprisal would be a single spark, one which would ignite the fire so carefully assembled by Samuel Roberts, the indomitable man of the people, and the much-respected voice of the working classes.

Part 2 – The Inevitable Spark

As with so many regrettable incidents from history, the spark was provided by another public menace – the intake of alcohol (ironically, a subject which Roberts had used in many of his essays), which was so often the catalyst of unfortunate events. On the evening of January 25 1835, just a few months after the publication of Roberts's damning pamphlet on the practices employed by the School of Anatomy, the caretaker of the very same building decided to finish his day with a trip to the local tavern. After being joined by a friend, the ale flowed rather more generously than previously intended, and an evening of relaxation soon turned into a night of terrible consequence – and a morning after that would eclipse even the mightiest hangover.

Staggering back to the school, with his drinking companion in tow, the caretaker eventually reached his living quarters having been jointly responsible for a number of ear-shattering crashes and bangs as the two men made their way through the dark corridors. No doubt angry at the drunken state of her husband, and the cacophony that had awoken her, the caretaker's wife emerged angrily in their living room, more than ready to give her inebriated spouse a considerable piece of her mind.

The caretaker took exception to her mood and, as he was in the company of his friend, no doubt felt embarrassment at the way he was greeted upon returning home. From this point, a blazing row ensued between the three. What followed is an appalling tale of violence, as the husband, having heard enough shouting for one night, began to beat his wife in front of his friend. Shamefully, the man, instead of preventing his companion from casting any further blows, joined in with the beating. Terrified and injured, the woman managed to free herself from the two men, and ran through the corridors in her nightdress, only stopping when she had safely emerged onto the city centre street, where she raised her head to the skies and screamed 'Murder! … Murder!'

The few people who were still roaming the street at that time of night were probably also under the influence of alcohol, a factor which certainly would not help when a bruised and bloody woman bursts through the doors of an Anatomy school screaming blue murder.

This was especially unfortunate given the recent events in which the school had been so publically questioned on its morality and unsavoury practices. As a result, this bizarre sight immediately garnered attention from those within hearing distance of the screams. Having been beaten, and breathless from the exertions of the last few minutes, the poor woman was unable to speak to those who surrounded her in the street, which resulted in her being unable to explain the situation, and before she regained her composure, a group of men had entered through the open door of the school. In what can only be imagined to be a sense of ale-fuelled bravado (as the interior of the Anatomy School was the last place most locals would want to explore by night), the men traversed the hallways and corridors of the building, and searched for signs of life as their eyes began to adjust to the darkness.

Unfortunately, what they would eventually find would not be signs of life, quite the opposite in fact. Their dark and fumbling reconnaissance had led them to an area of the school that was certainly not for the eyes of the public. They had found themselves in the belly of the beast. The sight that greeted this misguided band of explorers was one that would no doubt live within their memories for the rest of their lives. It was the stuff of nightmares, and given the unfamiliar surroundings, and the eerie darkness, it is no surprise that they did not wish to spend any more time in this godforsaken place.

The first discovery had been a human skeleton, gleaming in the moonlight as it hung grotesquely in the corner of a classroom, surveying the scene with the hollow apertures in which the windows of the soul, the eyes, should have been. Still reeling from this macabre vision, the men hurried from the classroom, only to take an unwise decision in which direction they should carry on, and found themselves in a place far more terrifying than the classroom and its fleshless occupant. They had unwittingly happened upon one of the school's dissection rooms, and were confronted by the sight of a sheet lying over a mysterious bulge, which lay upon a long ceramic table with deep indentations that ran the length of the unfamiliar piece of furniture. It should have been painfully obvious to the previously merry group that no good would come from giving in to curiosity and venturing further into the room, but at least one of them had decided to face their fear and seek what lay beneath the thick, heavy sheet.

Gingerly lifting the cover until their eyes could make out the object in the darkness, it was a matter of seconds before the men took the same course of action as the caretaker's wife had done just a short time before. Their emergence from the building was heralded by a crescendo of screams and cries as they ran back through the building, the volume rising considerably as they neared the front door, which still stood ajar. Those who had remained outside expected the men to emerge with the brutal attacker tightly in their grasp, but what they had emerged from the building with was a tale of horror and depravity, a story that would disgust and enrage the residents of Sheffield.

Beneath the sheet lay a corpse, which would have been frightening enough, had the corpse been in its complete state. However, as this particular corpse was currently being used as a research specimen, it was certainly not in a fit state to receive a viewing from anyone outside of the medical profession. The group of men had only lingered for a split second, but that was enough time to see with horror the cavernous open chest of the corpse, displaying its internal organs like some grotesque window display in a back street butcher shop.

By the time the men had emerged, the cause of the woman's screams had been established and relayed back to the hunting party, but their bravado had, all of a sudden, evaporated into the night air, and not one of these brave souls could be talked into returning back into the school. Instead, they breathlessly gave their accounts of the nightmarish scene that had confronted them as they had explored deeper into the bowels of the school, giving every detail, and possibly embellishing, the horrors they had discovered within. By now, the midnight cacophony had awoken everybody within earshot of the school, and groups of people stood shivering in the night air, passing on the information to each other as best they could. Meanwhile, those who strived to take control of the situation huddled together, and made a reckless and extremely unwise decision. They decided that the school should be closed for good, and the only way for that to be guaranteed was to destroy the very building that housed these monstrosities, and the devilish practices that took place behind those walls. However, as it was still the dead of night, it was resolved that any such action should wait until the morning, when daylight, and the aid of other local residents, would be available to assist this righteous group in their pursuits.

Very few of the massed residents were to sleep that night; instead, they nervously awaited the sunrise and, in the meantime, the story spread across the city, gathering more weight as it rolled along the streets, like a dirty, grey, snowball. There had long been stories pertaining to the reputation of one of the school's founders, Mr Wilson Overend, and his quest to rid any kind of premises of their recently departed occupants. Stories which, until now, had been (frustratingly, to those who opposed the school) completely unproven. Yet, as the old adage says, there can be no smoke without fire, and it would not be long before the smoke of these unfounded rumours was fuelled by its own fire; a fire that would be very real, and would change the face of Eyre Street forever.

Eventually, the chilling morning sky broke through the darkness, and it was to be on this day, 26January 1835, that a rebellion would take place; a rebellion created out of fear and ignorance, and one that would not be easily quashed.

Part 3 – Monday Morning Madness

The typical scene of 7am on a Monday morning in central Sheffield should have been very different. The residents should have been blearily making their way to their places of work, or to their schools. Yet, this particular Monday morning saw very little of these ordinary journeys being undertaken. Instead, groups of men and youths gathered quietly in the streets around the school, biding their time until the word was given to spring into action. A black mood still spread across the nearby streets, undoubtedly fuelled by anger and a lack of sleep. Women's faces then began to appear at the windows of the local houses, pressed to the frosty glass and with baited breath, they waited, motionless, until their husbands and sons suddenly leapt into action, and performed their duty in the face of this evil and sinful enemy.

This was nothing short of a military manoeuvre, with the amassed Sheffielders as the white knights, waiting to descend upon the walls of the seemingly impenetrable castle in which their friends and relatives were being cruelly, and godlessly, butchered under the very eyes of the law. And then it began, signalled not by some regal bugler, but by a working man whistling with his fingers between his teeth. The thirty-strong army merged as one, and approached the heavy wooden doors with an ever-gathering pace.

Previously concealed hammers and crowbars began to carve deep welts into the polished oak, each one seeking a point of leverage, or any gap in which the doors could be prised against their hinges. This struggle between man and manufacture was to last only a few minutes, as soon, with an almighty creak, the doors gave up their stubborn protest. The amassed ranks of outraged men filed into the building quickly and determinedly, like a line of ants, ready to carry out their duties with little or no regard for the establishment into which they had entered mob-handed. The few members of staff who had arrived at this early hour for their duties at the school exited the building in almost an exact reversal of the events of just moments ago, filing quickly, but with their heads held high, unwilling to show signs of fear in the face of their working class assailants.

It has not been documented whether the caretaker was one of those who escaped the building on this cold, grey morning, but as he was a permanent resident of the building, it is reasonable to assume that he was. If so, the hangover he must have been suffering that January morning would certainly be one to remember.

From outside the building, the sounds of chaos and destruction wafted across the icy street, coupled with interjections of discovery and encouragement from those inside. The hostile occupation of the building had not been enough; destruction was on the cards. It wasn't long before the windows burst into tiny crystals of broken glass, shattered from the inside by unknown hands and objects, the tiny fragments falling to the street where they mixed seamlessly with the early morning frost.

Then it began to rain. However, this was not the icy drizzle that one would have expected at this time of year; it was a rain of debris, which consisted of books, desks, broken furniture, and all kinds of medical equipment. By now it seemed that half of Sheffield had descended upon Eyre Street and, buoyed by the lack of opposition and the mood of camaraderie, more and more of the local men began to run through the broken doors to join their neighbours in the fight against their mutual enemy.

Judging by the amount of destroyed property that littered the street, and the jettisoning seeming to show no signs of slowing down, one could only imagine the scenes inside the building, which by now, must have been a broken-down skeleton of its former self. The wanton destruction carried on for a considerable amount of time before the local constables arrived to try and restore order. In fact, it was written in the notes of the first constable on the scene that he arrived at 9:30am – some two and a half hours after the doors had been breached.

Order was not to be restored however, as the approaching constables were deliberately held back by the crowd that had amassed around the building. There would be no interference until the job had been completed. Soon, to the great cheers of those gathered outside, smoke began to billow from one of the upstairs windows, winding its way into the icy morning sky, and growing ever thicker as the moments passed. Soon, flames could be seen licking at the empty window frames. The flames spread further across the upstairs windows, illuminating each one in turn, as the fire caught hold and charged its way through the building. Even by this stage, the billowing smoke could be seen for miles around. At this point, it would seem that the constables decided to give another push towards the building, but after one of them was struck by a brick thrown from the crowd, those remaining wisely opted for a strategy of self-preservation, and withdrew to a good distance away as they regrouped and waited for assistance.

By now, the downstairs windows had also become illuminated by the travelling flames, and danced brightly against the frosty backdrop of the early morning street. It would appear that the job in hand had almost been completed in its entirety. It was at this point that the local fire brigade arrived, charging into the crowd atop their horse-drawn wagons, and shouting at the assembled masses to move out of the way. Instantly, and shamefully, the firemen received the same treatment as the constables, and were soon retreating from a hail of stones and debris. By now the protest seemed unstoppable, and had long since reached riotous proportions. The police had failed to restore order, and the fire brigade were still prevented by the hostile crowd from performing their duties.

However, help arrived at almost exactly the moment that a group of local thugs had decided to overturn one of the horse-drawn fire engines. The whole scene froze instantaneously, and all stared sheepishly at the oncoming reinforcements. The military had arrived, armed with muskets and sabres, which were unsheathed and pointing at the mass of humanity that stood in their way. The Riot Act had been well and truly read, in both the figurative and literal sense, and this appeared to be the beginning of the end. Amongst this military procession stood a number of magistrates who were keen to catch a glimpse of the rabble rousers who would soon be standing before them, and to take in for themselves the scenes of this urban orgy of destruction and violence. The ring-leaders had already fled from the building and into the crowd as the fire had begun to spread. They were determined and angry, but not stupid. They would not meet their ends choked by acrid smoke in such a godless place. Forcing a path through the tangled limbs of those enjoying the spectacle, the military quickly ushered the fire brigade towards the building, where, protected and surrounded by soldiers, they went about the futile task of dousing the flames.

By early afternoon, the spectacle seemed to be over, and the streets had been cleared of everybody who wasn't involved in saving the remains of the building. A welcome hush had descended upon Eyre Street, and at this point, the military saw fit to withdraw. By 2pm however, the crowds had begun to assemble again, and the fire brigade, having succeeded in putting out most of the flames, now began to battle with a number of rioters who were intent on regaining access to the building.

Again, fires were started and the remaining walls and staircases pulled down by the tools of the protestors. This time however, the arrival of the military would not be a matter of hours, it would be a matter of minutes. The patience of the authorities had now been well and truly stretched, and without warning, the soldiers ran and rode towards the school, with weapons brandished, having been granted permission by the magistrates to restore order, whatever the cost.

Nobody stayed in the street for long enough to discover whether the military would really act upon the threats they bellowed as they approached. Like rats leaving a sinking ship, the rioters withdrew into the backstreets for their own safety and eventually returned home.

Yet, with the vast majority of the local population choosing not to attend their places of work that day, it would appear that the afternoon was a good one for the inn-keepers of central Sheffield, and by the time darkness descended above the still-smouldering school, a new target had been suggested. With misguided determination, and a lack of the correct information, a crowd descended upon the Sheffield School of Medicine, which lay just a few streets away from the smoke-filled skeleton of the Anatomy School. Little were the crowd aware that the Medical School and the Anatomy School were now, and had been for years, separate entities, with very different methods of research being performed in either school.

Yet, it would appear that the rioters saw the medical profession as the enemy, and with a beer-addled sense of duty, they arrived at the school armed with bricks and rocks, but unfortunately, not armed with the facts. Luckily, the crowd on this occasion was smaller than the one which had razed the Anatomy school to the ground just a few hours earlier, and as a consequence, gaining entry to the interior of the building was much harder work. Drunk and tired, these remaining rioters consoled themselves with launching their rocks and bricks at the windows of the school, shouting abuse into the night sky and waiting for reinforcements, which would, thankfully, never arrive.

The military, however, did arrive, and wasted no time in dispersing these persistent trouble-makers with very little regard to the concept of 'minimum force' and, bruised and bloody, the last remnants of the 1835 riot staggered home to sleep off the alcohol and tend their wounds.

Part 4 – The Aftermath

This was one of the last riots to take place in Britain in regards to the Anatomy Act, yet there would be further incidents, one of which would occur just a few miles northwest of Eyre Street, but more than a generation later.

It is easy to judge the actions of the rioters by today's standards, but one must remember that the fear of dissection and medical research was very real to the working classes during this time, and that their trust in the authorities was dubious to say the least.

As always, there were a number of people who revelled in the destruction and chaos, but most simply wanted to rid their city of a threat which was nightmarishly macabre, and went against every piece of religious dogma that they had been party to. It was, simply, a very unfortunate chain of events, which led all the way back to the seemingly innocuous legal battle which had been undertaken with vigour by Samuel Roberts in the late months of the previous year.

Ironically, it was to be Roberts himself who was the true victim of the whole ordeal, as it was the building he owned that was burned and gutted at the hands of the rabble he had tried so hard to rouse. The final bill for the damage to the School of Anatomy came in at £577 10s a monumental sum in 1835 (almost £30,000 in 2016). Eventually reimbursed by a mixture of insurance and compensation from the local council, Roberts never sought to rebuild the school and died just thirteen years later, having added no more essays to his portfolio.

The School of Anatomy returned to its previous tenancy within the Medical School on Surrey Street, from which it carried on its work, but in a more low-key and dignified manner than it had previously operated. No longer would they operate from the closed and clandestine environment of the Eyre street building. The founders of the school, most notably Mr Wilson Overend, were found to be completely innocent of any wrongdoing after it was proven beyond doubt that all cadavers used in their medical research were legitimately sourced and obtained, and could return to work with their reputations intact. In what can only be a fitting tribute for his part in bringing the medical trade out of the dark ages and into the light, a portrait of the other founding father of the School of Anatomy, Dr Corden Thompson, now hangs in the modern day Hallamshire Hospital.

This is a timely reminder that, without the financial and intellectual investment of men such as these, Sheffield would not enjoy such a glowing reputation in the study of medicine, and would not be home to the number of world class medical establishments which still grace the city today. As for the people of Sheffield themselves, their reaction to these extreme events varied, usually dependent on social class; a factor which is prevalent in most cases of civil unrest even today. It was rich against poor, educated against uneducated, and enlightened science versus archaic religion. Those who had vented their anger against the very building that stood for all they feared and abhorred, firmly believed that they acted with God on their side, subject as they were, to the religious dogma that often governed the lives and actions of the working classes. The educated minority, who had been lucky enough to have been exposed to the developments in modern science, acted with facts and progress on their side, and in the days following the ugly events, made their voices heard (usually anonymously) within the local press.

One thing that did unite many of the Sheffield residents during the ensuing clean-up operation was a shared sense of disappointment in the local constabulary. Their ineffectiveness at dispersing the crowds, and reliance on the brute force of the military was widely condemned. Many lives could have been lost if it were not for the sudden outbreak of common sense which washed over the crowd upon the arrival of the heavily armed local regiment, including those of the people who had attended the scene in order to assist with halting the unrest.

Below appears a letter, which appeared in the *Sheffield Independent* during the days following the riot; its contents amount to an angry attack on both the rioters, and the largely helpless constabulary. It appears in its entirety, and unsurprisingly, was submitted anonymously.

To the Editor of the Sheffield Independent;

Sir – I am truly astonished that such a contemptible and drunken scene, as occurred in Eyre Street, on Sunday and Monday last, should have been allowed to get to such a head as it did; and it should have been stopped after a few windows were broken.

I do not know the exact number of your constabulary and police force, but it must be considerable; and if they be active men, and of good nerve, they must have wanted a head to direct them, or this disgrace would not have fallen upon the town.

This circumstance will, I hope, cause your townsmen; with the population they have around them, to think about the propriety of having a magistrate always upon the place, aided by an effective and well-regulated police, by which this kind of effervescence, which will occasionally arise in all towns, but less in Sheffield, can be put down.

When a magistrate in this country does call out the military, they should be commanded by an officer higher than a sergeant.

I think the lower order of people, by rising and encouraging this spirit of hostility against improvement in the science of surgery etc, are pursuing a strangely infatuated course, and which will fall mainly upon themselves as they come to find out, if they have the misfortune to come under the hands of an unskilled and unpractised operator.

Yours faithfully,

Z

Many of the comments are fair, as it would be the working classes themselves who would suffer at the hands of poorly trained doctors, because those who could afford to avail themselves of a skilled doctor could be sure that their care would be provided by someone who had received every facet of medical training.

The doctors available to the poor would be nothing more than the traditional *barber surgeons*, who based their diagnoses on unproven remedies passed down through generations since the Dark Ages. At least the spread of dissection and anatomical study would be to their benefit as it would become commonplace in medical training.

The comments regarding the ineffectiveness of the police were also justified. At this time, the training available to a constable would largely consist of methods of physical restraint, rather than any kind of tactical or theoretical knowledge that would assist them under the varying situations in which they could find themselves. These comments mirrored the common opinion of the police during their early years, and the Sheffield constabulary were certainly to improve from this point onwards, most likely from the embarrassment of having to call in the military to restore order as the ineffective constables cowered from the crowds. No longer would policemen be burly *skull-crushers*, loitering on a street corner with truncheons swinging by their sides in preparation for the next drunkard or pickpocket. They would be part of a wider team, who, after some much needed training, would be able to assemble themselves as a unit in order to tackle any situation that may arise.

So, with a building razed to the ground, and a shameful stain on the reputation of the city, some green shoots did grow from the ruins of these events. The city would be better prepared for large-scale unrest, and the sense of safety for every resident would soon be greatly improved.

However, even with the School of Anatomy smouldering and destroyed, the majority would soon realise that they had ultimately been defeated, as the practice of anatomical study would spread until every medical school in the nation was furnished with its own dissection room. The head of the medusa had been temporarily lopped off, but in its place would grow several more, and as a result, the legal business of the medical schools, and the illegal practices of the resurrectionists, would continue for many years to come. Sadly, this would not be the last time that the city would be led to a frenzied outbreak of unrest at the hands of the resurrectionists, but for the present moment, everything had reverted to calm, and the people of Sheffield could return to their everyday lives.

Chapter 3

Take Them Up the Road

'Death doesn't change us more than life.'
Charles Dickens – The Old Curiosity Shop

Part 1 – The End of the Line

The life of a resurrectionist was far from glamorous, with cold nights spent shovelling frozen dirt, the necessary handling of lifeless corpses, and the constant threat of being apprehended. However, the trade could be very lucrative, and as such, many people of a less than honest persuasion would try their hand at the dark art of body snatching.

The trade was, of course, made possible by the paymasters who rewarded the resurrectionists handsomely for each cadaver they could supply. Usually working on behalf of a legitimate establishment, these respectable gentlemen were the last link in the chain of an extremely disreputable business. Yet, by the time the stolen corpses had arrived safely on the premises of the paymasters, the whole business had been laundered somewhat, and the middle class men of science could go about their gory tasks without fear of retribution, apart from the odd social uprising, which was usually quashed before getting out of hand.

The destruction of the medical school in Sheffield was very much an isolated incident, and was only brought about as false information had linked the school to playing a part in cold-blooded murder. Otherwise, the many centres of anatomical research that had sprung up around the nation were free to operate (no pun intended) as they pleased.

The main centre for anatomical research in the UK was Edinburgh, and as such, a large percentage of the disinterred corpses taken from British graveyards would eventually end up in the Scottish capital, especially those which had been obtained in the north of England. Owing to the laws of the land, especially those created to aid the medical profession, many of the corpses which ended up on the Scottish slabs were legally obtained, usually from the local workhouses or hospitals, or indeed anywhere that a penniless and unfortunate soul could meet their end.

Only London could rival Edinburgh for the sheer number of medical schools within its boundaries, and as such, the city was to receive far more than its share of large, unidentified packages, most of which arrived on courier coaches, always sent to a residential address, from where they would be transported on the last leg of their journey to the tradesman's entrances of the imposing University buildings.

As we are already aware, the city of Edinburgh was implicated in the scandal of Burke and Hare and their blossoming business, yet before the two Irishmen cast a permanent shadow over anatomical research within the city, the world of body snatching was only mentioned in hushed tones between the staff of the medical schools, and any civilian who had unwittingly witnessed these clandestine deliveries. By the time the Anatomy Act had been passed, and the schools were able to source their specimens from providers other than the local prisons, the calling for this distasteful trade began to boom.

Corpses from York, Leeds, Barnsley, Sheffield and Doncaster would all have ended up in Edinburgh, save for the small percentage that were used in medical schools closer to home, most notably in York or Sheffield. However, it was the preferred method of the resurrectionist to send their goods as far away as possible, thus weakening the ties between themselves and their lifeless cargo. The opportunists and small time body snatchers would often sell their wares to the nearest establishment, but those who had perfected the trade made sure to send their parcels north, as this is where the epicentre of their dark world lay. As such, there are many stories as to the participants of these eerie convoys, and we will now delve into the stories which document the journeys a number of these boxes took; many of which highlight the extent of this grotesque business, and the fortunes which could be made.

Part 2 – Boiled and Poached

The culprit in this story was something of a prolific resurrectionist, who would go on to commit more serious and notable crimes as time went by, and as such will also appear in a later chapter of this book, but in relation to a completely different story.

Here we look at the early work of a man who should have known better; a man who used his position of outward respectability, and his knowledge of the British legal system, to his advantage during a situation where any other member of working class society would have been hit by the full force of the law.

John Hodgson was a solicitor's clerk, and as such, was party to the goings-on of the local courthouses, especially when called upon to assist his employer during proceedings. It has been rumoured that Hodgson's penchant for body snatching was sparked by observing the lenient sentence handed out to one such individual, although this has never been confirmed.

The story begins with an event that stuck in the mind of a Leeds coachman, who, in May 1831, had been employed by three young men to transport them to Wortley, a district to the south of the modern city centre of Leeds; a normal enough occurrence for a coachman at this time. However, as the coach neared its destination, one of the three men called out to the driver to stop, and asked him to wait for their return, handing him a generous tip for his services. It was then that the coachman watched the three men walking across a field in the direction of a small churchyard, taking with them a large bag.

The bag flapped in the breeze as the group disappeared into the distance, yet when the three men returned; the bag was bulging, and was being carried by two of the men. This piqued the imagination of the driver, who wondered to himself what they could have possibly obtained from such a place, and in such a short time. Minding his own business, one of the defining characteristics of a hired river, the man thought nothing more about this strange event as he guided his horses back to Leeds, and concentrated upon the track before them, leaving his passengers to engage each other in quiet conversation. Before long however, the men began to bicker amongst themselves, seemingly in regards to where the mysterious cargo would be taken upon their return. One of the men, who appeared to be the most dominant, eventually gave the driver his instructions. They were to be taken to the office of a well-known solicitor, Mr Gaunt. The driver continued to eavesdrop on the rest of the conversation during the short trip back to Leeds, and was surprised to hear the men referring to the cargo as 'the subject' on several occasions. Dropping his passengers off at their final destination, the coachman spent the rest of the day pondering their conversation, but by the time he returned home, other matters had occupied his mind, and the unusual trip had lost its place at the forefront of his memory.

The story now reverts to a horrific event which had taken place just days before, a story which soon intertwines with the three men in the carriage and their mysterious bag. As ghastly as this story is, it will get much worse as the connection becomes apparent. Leeds was home to a large number of weavers and mills, and employment in these industries was the main factor in the rapid expansion of the city. However, the safety of employees during the nineteenth century was rarely something that was considered by the mill owners and, as such, a large proportion of the workforce would experience some kind of accident during their working life. Tim Rothery had worked in such a mill since his teens, and had, until now, managed to avoid any serious accident whilst performing his job as a dyer, which involved large vats of red hot liquid, and no protective clothing whatsoever. Therefore, it was on the cards that Rothery would one day meet with danger. Unfortunately, the accident that was to befall him would also prove fatal, and result in an agonising and slow death, whilst onlookers could only close their eyes and ears to the screams of their colleague.

At some point during his working day, Rothery had gone up onto a wooden gantry in order to stir one of the vats of dye, a task he had undertaken many times a day since the first day of his employment. On this day however, he would never climb down the steps to safety, and would not return home to his family. Somehow, the unfortunate dyer managed to lose his footing whilst stirring the mixture, and plunged head first into the bubbling vat. His screams of agony could be heard the length of the building until the pain of the extensive scalding was too much to bear and Rothery, thankfully, lost consciousness before he was finally consumed by the boiling liquid. As causes of industrial death go, this must be one of the most painful, and easily one of the most difficult to witness because, within seconds of the accident occurring, there is no way in which anybody can assist the unfortunate victim.

A funeral was arranged, and paid for by the owner of the mill, which was an unusual gesture during these days of unprotected servitude. Many friends and colleagues joined the family in saying farewell to Tom Rothery, who was a popular character at home and at work, and prayed for his soul to be accepted into heaven, relieving him of the pain he had endured during his death. Little did anybody know that at least one of the mourners had attended the funeral for a very specific reason; a reason which would add insult to the injury sustained by Rothery, and cause a whole new chapter of grief for his bereaved family. Two days later, the grave that held the scalded remains of the dyer was found to be in disarray, and an investigatory dig revealed that the body had been removed from the grave by means of being dragged through a hole made in the upper portion of the casket.

The police were immediately called for, and investigations into the theft of the body began. However, with very little to go on, it was decided that the best course of action would be to release the details of the crime, hoping that a witness would be able to shed some light on the abhorrent crime that had been committed. It is at this point that the two stories become one, as the inquisitive coachman read the morning papers before heading out to work. The location of the crime, and that to which he transported the three young men, were very close, and the mysteriously bulging bag only added to his misgivings. Paying a visit to his local constable, the coachman recounted the strange journey on which he had embarked two days previously, describing every detail that could have been of use to the police in their enquiries. The most important piece of information to be provided was not the description of the three men, or the details of their conversation, but the location in which the journey ended, as this gave the police a starting point from which to begin the investigation.

The following morning, a small detachment of constables arrived unannounced at the business premises of the respected Mr Gaunt armed with a search warrant. Ever the law abiding citizen, Gaunt immediately granted access and apologised that the constables would have to perform their search unescorted, as his clerk had failed to report for work that morning. Convinced that they would find nothing amiss, the policemen went about their search nonetheless, and were about to bid farewell to Mr Gaunt when one of the constables located a concealed area, used as a lumber hole, which was tucked away in the recess beneath the stairs. A cursory peer into the recess was enough to confirm the presence of a large box, on which had been attached a note reading 'Books – Please keep dry', although, it was obvious from the sickly-sweet and nauseating smell that had greeted the nostrils of the constable who entered the space that the contents of this box did not belong in a library.

The sight that greeted the police upon opening the box was one of such horror that none of them would ever forget the moment. A decomposing corpse is bad enough, but one covered in pus-filled blisters is something entirely worse. The general state of the body, especially in conjunction with the information provided by the coachman, left no doubt that the appalling sight before them was nothing other than the decaying corpse of the unfortunate Tom Rothery.

The description of the three young men as provided by the coachman were related to Mr Gaunt, who immediately, and with great regret, confirmed that the man who was identified as the 'dominant' man was none other than John Hodgson, the clerk who had failed to attend work. Gaunt, who was now in an absolute state of shock after finding a decaying corpse under his stairs and discovering that his trusty clerk was responsible, described Hodgson as being intelligent, respectable and loyal, not quite the traits one would normally use to describe a resurrection man.

A bulletin was immediately put out across the whole of Yorkshire, and it was not long before a courier arrived from Harrogate, bearing a letter which informed the Chief of West Yorkshire police that Hodgson had been identified and apprehended in Harrogate earlier that morning. With very little to offer in way of a defence, Hodgson was, however, successful in persuading his employer to represent him in court, something which shows the regard in which the dutiful clerk had been previously held.

Yet, despite his adequate representation, Hodgson elected to undertake most of his defence by himself, a decision seriously questioned by his employer, who was ultimately unable to persuade his employee to change his mind. Hodgson's unusual defence was that he freely admitted to taking the body, but had only done so in order to practice the art of dissection, as he had a long-term ambition to become a surgeon. He was adamant that he never intended to sell the body for profit. His intention was to not only defend himself, but to defend the whole process of dissection; an art which he claimed was invaluable to the future of medical science, and which had been freely accepted in other countries, which threatened to overtake Britain as the centre of the medical world.

Addressing the magistrate directly at the outset of his hearing, Hodgson adamantly informed the court that 'it is nature that teaches us to use the bodies of the dead to preserve the bodies of the living', an argument which was accepted as legitimate by the magistrate. Even the prosecutor was in agreement with Hodgson in principle, but challenged the act of removing a body from the churchyard without permission or qualification, to which Hodgson retorted, asking how else a layman would be able to access a corpse for dissection. The defendant went on to explain how he would have dissected the body in the company of a friend of his, who was a medical student at a Leeds establishment, but refused to name this friend, as he stated 'I could not give his name without utterly ruining him.'

The case was adjourned for sentencing, and during the hiatus, the mere mention of the Leeds medical school caused much unrest amongst the citizens of Leeds, who mentally tied the events together, and came up with the conclusion that the educational establishment was somehow complicit in this grotesque business. This resulted in the brother of Tom Rothery being arrested for an altercation with Robert Baker, the chief surgeon of the Leeds School of Anatomy. This was quickly resolved after an apology was issued by the livid Rothery sibling, who then apologised in return for his freedom.

By the time the court case had restarted, Hodgson had even managed to find three members of the medical profession who would speak on his behalf. This was a stroke of genius on the part of Hodgson, as each and every ally of reputable standing would legitimise his defence. One such testimony came from William Wildsmith, a respected surgeon who informed the court that anyone who aimed to become a surgeon could not progress without dissecting at least one corpse; his opinion was shared by another two character witnesses, both of whom claimed that Hodgson was extremely skilled for a layman, and would make a fine surgeon in the future. It was on this statement that the whole defence hinged, with Hodgson earnestly imploring the court to spare him from conviction, as his future prospects would be ruined by a spell of incarceration, especially over such a controversial matter.

The magistrate accepted Hodgson's well-thought-out argument, and also concurred that he was prepared to accept that Hodgson had no intention of selling the body for profit. However, a crime had been committed, and the people of Leeds would demand some punishment in recompense. Sentencing Hodgson to a short six-week stint in York Castle gaol, the magistrate did reassure the prisoner that such a short sentence was unlikely to have any adverse effect upon his ambition to practice as a surgeon, especially if he were to study in some place other than Leeds.

All of this begs the question, was Hodgson's defence genuine? Or was it a clever ruse by an intelligent man who was desperate to avoid a lengthy prison sentence? Many factors can be looked into, such as the claim that the dissection would only have taken place in the company of a registered surgeon, and in the company of a number of medical students, which poses the quandary, why steal a corpse in the first place?

Surely if Hodgson was so well regarded by the medical profession, he could have asked to attend a dissection within the medical school itself, especially as he seemed to be on such good terms with those in charge of the establishment. Also, why hide the body in the premises of his employer (who re-employed Hodgson as soon as he completed his prison sentence)? Surely the body would have been taken to his home if the dissection was to take place in a private venture?

One factor unknown to the magistrate was that Hodgson had previously spent a large amount of time in Edinburgh, the dissection capital of the western world, and had become acquainted with several employees who worked for the flourishing medical schools there. Indeed, it was rumoured that Hodgson learned the skills of the resurrectionist whilst in the Scottish capital, and had previously sold a number of cadavers to the anatomists – something that was to be confirmed in a future court case.

The most likely explanation would be that Hodgson had intended the body to be transported to Edinburgh, and had stored the box at his employer's premises due to its close proximity to the courier coach office, and also to distance himself from the incriminating item if it was to be discovered. It would have been easy to send the box on its way up the Great North Road, and to wait for remuneration to be sent by post, therefore avoiding any involvement with the Leeds medical schools in which he hoped to one day study.

The truth will never be established, but later events in which Hodgson featured as the main protagonist would suggest that this was a far more wicked act than was presented to the court.

Part 3 – Room at the Inn

As is highlighted in the story of John Hodgson's early foray into the world of the resurrectionist, one problem which would often prove tricky to those in the trade, was that of finding a suitable place for storage until the ill-gotten gains could be safely transported to their final destination. One solution, which seems to have been especially popular in the north of England, was to befriend an innkeeper, who would allow items to be stored within the pub cellar for a small charge. This was especially beneficial if the inn in question was also a coaching inn.

A striking example of this arrangement took place in the heart of the Yorkshire Dales, a remote and beautiful area of the country, but one which holds many of the same dark secrets as one would discover when delving into the history of much more populous settlements. This particular story takes place in the stunning wilderness of Wensleydale, where one such tavern was popular for a number of reasons: the friendly landlord, the quality of the ale, and the availability of storage for any cadavers you may be transporting north to Edinburgh.

The Black Swan in the village of Leyburn was built in the seventeenth century, and became popular as a place of accommodation and sustenance for cross-country travellers who found themselves riding through the quiet countryside of the Yorkshire Dales. The location of the inn was particularly handy for those who were travelling from west or south Yorkshire towards the North, the very same route taken by several pieces of cargo that had previously been in the possession of some of Yorkshire's resurrectionists.

Unfortunately, no detailed accounts of particular cases were ever documented, but local legend has it that the inn was used by several courier coach companies, whose drivers could be persuaded to add an extra item to their wagon in return for a mug of ale and a bowl of stew. Also well documented was the voluminous size of the tavern's cellars, which stretched well below the outside walls of the building and into the subterranean caverns below and proved ideal for the storage of any perishable items.

As you have no doubt already concluded, the landlord of this particular inn during the early to mid-nineteenth century was not averse to making an extra few pounds each month and, as such, was particularly receptive to those who wished to rent part of his cellar for a night or two. An account from the time describes the cellar as being cold and dry, and containing a number of slabs which had been made from local stone and laid flat in regular intervals throughout the far recesses of the sizeable chamber. Legend has it that instruction was given to certain coach drivers to make their overnight halt at the Black Swan, and to store certain large boxes in the cellar until the morning, when the journey would be recommenced.

One particular story, which unfortunately does not exist on paper, but was told to me by an elderly former resident of nearby Bellerby, is as entertaining as it is ghastly, and thoroughly deserves its place within this compendium. It begins with a coachman who arrived at the inn in order to make an overnight stop, and paid the few pennies to rent a room before unloading his cargo into the cellar, as instructed by the sender who paid the courier extra to ensure that his large box was kept out of sight and in the cool of the deep cellar. As only one box had been earmarked for special treatment, and happened to be at the bottom of the pile of boxes heading for Edinburgh, the coachman (who was used to delivering this kind of 'special' delivery) had no choice but to fully unload his wagon, before placing the remaining items back on board.

The night passed without incident; in the morning, the courier reclaimed the box from the cellar, and loaded it back onto the wagon. Unfortunately, during the loading and reloading, some of the address labels had become detached from their respective boxes but, after a brief moment of panic, the courier was satisfied that he had the situation in hand, and merrily recommenced his journey.

Upon reaching Edinburgh two days later however, the courier realised that he only had two boxes left to deliver, and that both were of similar size and weight. He had no choice but to establish which box held the 'special' cargo, and which contained an innocent object bound for the Scottish capital. As luck would have it, the first box to be opened contained – to the courier's relief – a set of drawers, wrapped in carpet to protect them from the bumps and bangs of a four-day wagon journey. This meant that the remaining box would, thankfully, not need to be opened.

When the boxes had finally been delivered, and the medical school had received their important box, the driver began his journey south, along with a new cargo of boxes and packages bound for the towns and cities of Yorkshire. Two days later, the driver once again arrived at the Black Swan and approached the landlord to request a room for the night, at which, the landlord became irate and told the courier to find somewhere else to stay in future. When questioned as to the reason for his hostility, the innkeeper took the coachman down to the cellar, and pointed at a box which was resting upon one of the stone slabs shouting 'that's the bloody problem!'

Confused as to what had happened, the courier realised that the box was similar in size and weight to the box he had delivered to the medical school, and the colour drained from his face as he realised what had happened. Unbeknown to the courier, the innkeeper had also been storing a box in the cool of the cellar; it was that box containing a delivery of meat intended to last for the next week that had been delivered to the medical school. Pulling the top from the box and exposing the grisly contents, the innkeeper shouted angrily 'do you want me to put *that* in the bloody stew?' before turning on his heels and storming up the cellar steps.

After a moment of contemplation, the courier followed the innkeeper into the snug, and offered to pay the full price of the meat that had been taken, to which the innkeeper smiled and said 'that's all very well, but I hope the doctors can learn plenty from my side of beef!' before laughing at the look of absolute horror on the face of the inept courier.

It is impossible to ascertain whether there is any truth in this story, but I'm sure I'm not the only one who hopes that this really happened, and that the courier didn't get into too much trouble for delivering a very large mixed grill to the Edinburgh School of Anatomy.

Chapter 4

Resurrection Cottage

'Doctors are just the same as lawyers; the sole difference being that lawyers only rob you, whereas doctors rob you and kill you too.'

Anton Chekov – Ivanov

Part 1 – Mills and Boom

One of the most daring and prolific of Yorkshire's resurrection men to use the convenient Roman road from York to Edinburgh was a resident of nearby Leeds, a relatively close neighbour to the bodysnatching hotspot of York, which lies just twenty-seven miles to the northeast, and easily within a day's journey by horse and cart.

Leeds, like York, was already a thriving city by the nineteenth century, and was undoubtedly the second most populous area of Yorkshire although, despite its long and impressive history, the city could never match York in terms of grand architecture or historic importance.

The history of Leeds can be traced back to the fifth century, when it received several mentions in documents of the day as a wooded and rural area, highly valued for fertile farmland and its convenient central position within the north of England. The name of the city derives from the word 'Ladenses', referring originally to almost the whole of West Yorkshire, and meaning 'people of the fast-flowing river'. The River Aire still flows through the heart of the city today, and was crucial in playing a part in the development of modern day Leeds.

From the thirteenth century onwards, Leeds was made up of small farming communities, which eventually expanded until they began to rub shoulders, at which point the area became a lively and thriving market town and a popular place to stay for travelling armies and trades people. The real growth, however, was to come during the Industrial Revolution, when the

River Aire was able to power the countless mills built upon its banks, all of which were able to produce wool quickly and cheaply, ensuring that plenty of steady work was available to the townsfolk, and that Leeds would not be left behind other developing towns such as Sheffield and Barnsley. Even more beneficial was the mammoth building project that was the Leeds and Liverpool Canal, which ensured that passing trade would always be available to the town, and that there would be ample provision for the supply and demand needs of the busy mills.

Despite its development and geographical importance, especially during the nineteenth century, it is fairly strange to note that the area seems to have been relatively untouched by scandal or public unrest, something that was uncommon for a large settlement, especially during the Victorian era, in which every city seemed to have some kind of macabre tale to tell. Yet, there is one dark tale that lies hidden within the secret history of Leeds: a tale of opportunistic crimes and immoral acts. In terms of the grim history of the anatomists, this is one of the most jaw-dropping tales of all.

One of the defining characteristics of the resurrection men (apart from the notable exception of the infamous Burke and Hare, and they operated with very different, and murderous, *modus operandi*), is that in almost every case, they worked alone. Leeds was unfortunate enough to be home to four such men, all of whom worked in tandem to streamline their ghastly operations, a trait which is extremely uncommon in the annals of body snatching, and resulted in a clandestine, yet booming, business.

To say that the four men must have trusted in each other is an understatement, because the reason the vast majority of resurrection men worked alone is that, in this line of business it was very difficult to trust anyone; even the families of the body snatchers were usually kept in the dark as to the source of their unexplained extra income.

Yet, John Hodgson (a solicitor's clerk, who appears in an earlier chapter, such was his prolific career), John Wood (shoemaker), James Pickering (schoolmaster), and James Norman (butcher) operated as a successful team, each of them using their respectable outward appearances to aid them in carrying out their macabre work without fear of discovery. Such was the professionalism of their operation that the men had even rented premises in which to go about their ungodly work. This was crucial in keeping their activities away from the prying of eyes of not just the local residents, but also their own families, who remained blissfully unaware of the night-time occupations of their patriarchs.

The detached house, which was situated on Tobacco Mill Lane in the Sheepscar area of the city, was innocuous enough at the time not to have caused anyone to question the depraved acts that were organised and carried out inside; yet this building would soon be known to everyone in the local area, and would be chillingly referred to as *'Ressurection Cottage.'*

It is unclear as to how long this little business had been in operation but, given that the four men had infrequently attended the cottage for almost two months during the early winter of 1831, it is safe to say that trade had been good enough to allow for the expense of hiring the premises, and would suggest that their secret occupations had long since been mastered. The building was large enough for the four men to operate in relative comfort, but not big enough to draw the attention of any onlooker who would question the sporadic use of the house. If it had not been for a business opportunity that befell the owner of the cottage, one can only imagine how many unfortunate people would have suffered their earthly remains being processed through this lucrative venture.

Part 2 – A Respectable Façade

Mr William Peniston, the owner of the house, had rented the property to James Pickering, a schoolmaster with impeccable references (and probably the most outwardly respectable member of the four-man gang) since October 1831, and had been given no cause to suspect that any nefarious activities were taking place under his roof. However, the arrangement had only been in place for just over a month before Peniston was approached by a local couple, Mr and Mrs Evans, who had expressed a serious interest in purchasing the property for a good price, thus leaving Peniston with a dilemma – allow Pickering to continue his tenancy, or sell the premises to the Evanses.

As would be expected, the draw of a large sum of money appealed to Peniston, and as he had no firm contract with Pickering, he decided to pursue the opportunity of the sale. All that was left to do was to inform Pickering of the awkward news, and arrange a viewing for the keen, and obviously wealthy, Mr and Mrs Evans. However, despite his tenant taking the news well, and vowing that he would not stand in the way of the sale, Peniston did come up against considerable difficulty when trying to arrange the viewing he had promised to the prospective buyers. His messages to Pickering went unanswered, and it was almost a week before he tracked down the schoolmaster and was able to make arrangements face to face. The first attempt to enter the premises was unsuccessful however, because Pickering (who was not to accompany the landlord and the Evanses during the viewing) claimed that he did not have the keys. As this was the only set, Pickering promised to meet with the viewing party at a later date to arrange entry.

The elusive keys finally appeared on 7 November, yet this was far from ideal, as Mr Evans was previously engaged. Mrs Evans did manage to take a look around the house, accompanied by Peniston and a Mr William Myers, a friend of Peniston who had introduced the couple to the landlord upon hearing that they were in the market for a house.

As Mr Evans had been unable to attend, the visit proved largely fruitless, as Mrs Evans could not, and would not, make a decision without her husband being present. Also hampering the sale was the fact that a large upstairs closet was firmly locked, and the key for this had not been provided by Pickering. Questioning Pickering about the missing key, the landlord was satisfied that his tenant would return that evening with it, and this would allow Mr Evans time to return to Sheepscar in order to make a proper viewing along with his wife. All parties seemed satisfied by this resolution.

That evening, Peniston and Myers arrived early at the house, having decided to make one last check of the premises before the decisive viewing. Waiting in the doorway was Pickering, who appeared agitated and flushed. Trying in vain to stall the two men with conversation, Pickering eventually moved aside to allow entry, before quickly turning and walking away with a considerably quicker gait than would have been expected. Undeterred by this unusual behaviour, Peniston and Myers began the inspection of the house from the ground floor. However, as they moved through the downstairs room, they were alerted to a series of bangs and creaks from the upstairs. They were not alone in the house, and were quick to investigate this unexpected occurrence. By the time the two men had reached the hallway, they were astounded to witness the sight of three men bundling a large box on a sack barrow down the last few stairs, before making for the door with extreme haste, and not a single word of explanation.

Dumbstruck by the events which had just unfolded, Peniston and Myers watched open-mouthed for a moment, as the three men hurried along the street with their bulky burden; coincidentally, in the exact same direction taken by Pickering just a few minutes before. On regaining their composure, the first reaction of the landlord and his friend was to assume that a robbery had just taken place, one organised by a disgruntled ex-tenant, who had also disappeared into the sunset following their awkward exchange outside the premises.

Being outnumbered, Peniston and Myers made a quick decision to follow the three men from a safe distance, rather than to give chase and risk being subjected to an attack. As they made their way through the streets, keen not to lose sight of their prey, the destination of the men and their mysterious haul quickly became apparent. In fact, as they reached the journey's end of a Courier coach parked next to the Rose and Crown Inn on Briggate, it became clear that Pickering certainly was involved, as he waited impatiently by the coach for the three men to join him and send their haul onwards to the intended destination.

With impeccable timing, a police constable strolled past the two hidden observers at that very moment, and was immediately informed of the strange events that had just taken place. By this point, the coach was ready to leave, and the large box was almost on board, being wrestled into position by the burliest of the four men who were so interested in seeing their package off.

Constable William Halton ordered the coachman to remain stationary, and took hold of the burly man, the butcher, James Norman. Unfortunately, upon seeing the oncoming constable, the three other men had fled into the distance; so much for a brotherly bond between thieves. Sounding his whistle for assistance, it was a matter of moments before two other constables arrived to assist in the investigation by keeping a firm grip on the butcher, giving Constable Halton opportunity to inspect the clandestine cargo and its contents.

The address label read 'Hon. Ben Thompson, mail Office, Edinburgh. To be kept until called for. Per courier, Nov 7th, 1831'. Still none the wiser as to its contents, (the butcher was certainly not giving any answers Constable Halton called to the coach driver for a tool which could prise open the lid of the box. Immediately, a chisel was produced by the driver, who was still confused at being stopped by the police in his day-to-day business, and the lid was forcefully removed. Inside, covered by packing straw, lay the body of a young man.

Quickly replacing the lid of the box, in order to prevent a riot amongst the crowds that had gathered around the coach, keen to observe this unusual police investigation, Constable Halton immediately ordered that Norman be taken to the police station by his colleagues, and began to enquire as to whether anyone could identify the three men who had melted away into the city centre. Several members of the gathering crowd were certain that the man who had waited by the coach was none other than the schoolmaster, Mr Pickering. This was also confirmed by the coach office, which informed the constable that transit had been paid for by Mr Pickering, and the address label had been filled in by his own educated hand.

With Norman in custody, and the box safely taken away to the police station for safekeeping, Halton's next port of call was to be the elegant tenements of Bond Street, of which the professional bachelor, the respected schoolmaster Mr James Pickering, was a long-term resident. Obviously unaware that he could have been identified so easily, Pickering had indeed returned to his rooms in Bond Street, and was present when Constable Halton hammered upon his door less than half an hour after his forced escape from the Rose and Crown Coaching Inn. With no means of escape, Pickering had no choice but to open the door to the policeman, who immediately identified that Pickering was not alone. In the room with him, lounging in a chair, was John Craig Hodgson, a man who was certainly not a stranger to the macabre trade of the resurrectionist. With the two men quickly removed from the premises, and taken without a struggle to the police station in order to be brought before the Chief Constable, Halton was able to make a quick search of the rooms, and in so doing, uncovered a very telling collection of items.

In plain sight lay wet and muddy clothing, a length of rope, a crowbar, two spades, a saw and a gimlet. These were certainly the tools of the trade that would be in the possession of any resurrectionist, and the dampness of the filthy clothing indicated that they had been used fairly recently.

Meanwhile, at the police station, the two recently disturbed men were being interrogated by the Chief Constable, but had greeted this questioning with an impenetrable wall of silence. However, for one man at least, the records of his previous exploits were about to speak a thousand words.

Hodgson's file was on the desk of the Chief Constable, and was recent enough to show no signs of wear and tear this was a recently created criminal record, and the paperwork within was astonishingly similar to that which would soon be added. Just four months before this incident, Hodgson had been arrested for the theft of a body, and, as we know, had been sentenced to six weeks imprisonment (the lenient sentence being commonplace in regards to a crime which officially did not exist in the eyes of the law) for desecration of a grave. Whereas previously, the solicitor's clerk had claimed that he had taken the corpse purely for his own research, and had no intention of profiting from this distasteful act, this time Hodgson could not rely on this explanation, because it had already been established that the body was to be conveyed to Edinburgh.

The two were reunited in the cells with James Norman, and John Wood, the last of the four to be apprehended. The shoemaker had also been identified by an eyewitness and, like Pickering and Hodgson, had assumed that their getaway had been successful, and returned to his premises to lie low for a while. To the Chief Constable, the mechanics of the gang were becoming clear. Hodgson was the leader and used his experience to source new corpses to disinter, Pickering was the respectable face of the gang, and Norman and Wood were the muscle, tasked with taking on the majority of the heavy and dirty work.

Part 3 – The Sad Tale of Robert Hudson

Meanwhile, the body had been moved to Leeds Infirmary for post-mortem, a necessary procedure in a case such as this, as the cause of death must be established before an inquest can take place. Surgeon Thomas Chorley was tasked with this unpleasant act, and began by making a very shrewd observation as to the state of the corpse before him. The cadaver was filthy, yet fresh, which led Chorley to infer that the body had never been buried, as part of the funeral arrangements would have been the washing and preparing of the body before burial. This suggested a very serious development in the case, one which could lead to four more corpses finding their way to the anatomist operating tables.

However, by reason of his profession, Hodgson was allowed to speak with Chorley and, in a meeting that is reported to have lasted for over two hours, was able to satisfy himself that the surgeon, despite his previous misgivings, was unable to establish any unnatural causes relating to the death of the man. Suicide had been given as the official cause of death. This, no doubt, calmed the nerves of Hodgson and his gang; to take a body was one thing, but to murder a person in order to take possession of their corpse was an entirely different state of affairs, and could have seen the gang hanged for their involvement in such a crime.

So, the body was removed to the courthouse, and was displayed for public viewing in the hope that somebody would be able to identify the unfortunate man, and may be able to offer further information as to the reason for the state of the corpse and the circumstances surrounding his death. A description was also printed in the *Leeds Patriot and Yorkshire Advertiser*.

A Young Man, about 18 Years of Age, Five Feet Six Inches high, Face slightly round, Brown Hair, cut short behind, and long before, slightly calf licked on the right side of the Head, very short down Beard, with scarcely any Whiskers; the left Incisor Tooth stands backward, and the left Canine Tooth forwards.

Blue Eyes, of which the left is somewhat injected with Blood; rather fair Complexion, well made and somewhat muscular; the Nail of the ring Finger of the right Hand has been destroyed, and a new Nail partially formed; a slight graze on the right shin nearly healed; there is dirt on the Legs set into the Skin, and the Body exhibits no appearance of illness.

The decision to exhibit the body to the public soon paid off, as a friend of the deceased was able to identify the body as being of Robert Hudson, a collier who hailed from the district of East Ardsley. Hudson's family were sent for in order to confirm this identification, and very soon, Robert's brothers, Joseph and John arrived, and confirmed without doubt that this was the corpse of their younger brother. While the two brothers were engaged in completing the necessary paperwork, a party of police constables was dispatched to the East Ardsley graveyard in order to establish that the grave was, indeed, empty. It did not take long to establish this as being the case. The coffin, which was now half filled with earth, had been sawn open from head to chest, with holes having been drilled into the corners of the aperture in order to aid in the sawing of the wood. The corpse had indeed gone, and the contents of the casket were nothing more than a glove and an iron bar, which had been left behind by the gang of desecrators.

As this discovery was being made, another important piece of information was being relayed at the police station, as the two Hudson brothers told the story of how their younger sibling came to be buried in such a filthy state, and at such a tender age. The last anyone had seen of 17-year-old Robert Hudson was at around 11am on 30 October, at which time he left the home of his mother, after paying a morning visit. No more sightings of Hudson were made after this, until his body was discovered in a cabin at the coal pit where he was employed. Robert Hudson had committed suicide, hanging himself from a beam inside the cabin with his neckerchief. No tangible reason could be offered for this terrible event. No note had been left, and the family were unaware of any reason as to why their youngest member would take his own life in such a lonely and squalid place. The local inquest, which had taken place the next day, recorded a verdict that Hudson had 'hung himself while in a state of unsound mind.' The burial was arranged to take place the very next day, and the notes entered into the burial records stated 'hung himself in a coal pit cabin'.

It was only eight years before this tragic death that the 1823 Burial of Suicide Act had been passed, allowing the burial of someone who had taken their own life to take place within the consecrated grounds of a churchyard. However, not all of the traditional facets of a church funeral were to take place in such a case.

The burial would occur without a church service, and could only be undertaken between the hours of 9pm and 12am. This was commonplace in the case of a suicide, as the church, although willing to perform the public service of a burial, would not allow the coffin to enter the church itself, and would not open the funeral to the public.

Part 4 – The Completed Jigsaw

This sad story did solve two rather pressing puzzles. Firstly, the freshness of the corpse is explained by the fact that the coffin had only been buried a matter of a few hours before the gang had arrived to disinter Robert Hudson, whose body would be as valuable to them as it was useless in the eyes of the church. Secondly, the filthy corpse had not been washed or prepared, as the services of an undertaker were never called for, such was the nature of this particular burial. The dirt on the body was the very same blackness that had covered the surfaces of the coal pit cabin where Hudson was to spend the final moments of his life. This at least exonerated Hodgson and his gang from the serious charges which could have been faced if it were not for the diligence of the surgeon who performed the post-mortem, but other events that had since taken place were now firmly shoving the taboos of body snatching closer to the gang every minute.

Four more men had been apprehended, after it was suspected that they had also taken part in the creation and growth of this thriving resurrectionist business. William Germaine (packer), William Bradley (joiner), Thomas Pearson (weaver), and Henry Teale (gentlemen's servant) had also been regular visitors to the house on Tobacco Mill Lane. Keen to protect his reputation, and in an effort to save himself from imprisonment, Henry Teale immediately took the offer of a bargain with the police, and during the court proceedings which took place on 14 November, laid out the details of the case for the assembled jury.

Hodgson was indeed the ringleader and the brains behind the operation. He had hand-picked his gang over the previous months, and on the day of the incident had given Teale a list of churchyards in which were believed to be easy-pickings, and asked him to make a note of any recent burials. Teale reported to Hodgson that there were two new graves, one large, and one small. Both were targeted by Hodgson for disinterment, and on that very same evening, Hodgson, Bradley, Germaine and Teale hired two carts, and set off for East Ardsley in darkness.

Upon reaching the graveyards, Hodgson stood on the perimeter of the grounds, armed with two pistols, which Teale explained he would have had no qualms about using, should the gang have been disturbed during their moonlit toils. The other three men took turns to dig down into the cold winter soil and, before long, the two bodies were unearthed, one being the corpse of Robert Hudson, and the other being the remains of 4-year-old Joseph Longley, who had also been buried that day.

The police inspection of the churchyard (which did not spot the crude re-filling of the Longley grave) discovered that the bodies had been accessed by sawing through the upper portion of the coffins, the corpses were then dragged from the ground by use of a rope around the neck. All linen was removed and placed back into the graves, as the theft of these items was more serious in the eyes of the law than the disinterment of the corpses themselves! Placed into separate sacks, the bodies were put onto the carts, and the gang, after re-filling the graves, quickly and quietly began their journey back to the busier streets of central Leeds, where the corpses would be initially placed in readily prepared boxes, and stored in an outhouse belonging to Norman's father (who was unaware of the contents of these boxes).

Just a few hours later, the bodies were removed in order for them to be placed on the early morning courier coach, yet the gang had made a serious error. They had decided to take a short nap before taking the boxes to the coach, and arrived too late, the coach having left just moments before. The boxes were taken back to the outhouse, but after a friendly inquisition by Norman's father, the gang decided that their haul was no longer safe there, and took measures to avoid the elder Mr Norman becoming even more inquisitive.

The box of the child was placed on the next available coach, but the gang were still stuck with the larger box, which would not fit upon this particular conveyance, and would have to be taken back to the place in which the gang met to discuss their plans, the house on Tobacco Mill Lane.

A second attempt was made the next morning, but after being informed that the coach was already full, the box was taken back, and stored in an upstairs closet – the very closet that Mr Peniston and Mrs Evans found locked during their visit. In sheer desperation, the gang had stored their bounty in the closet right until the last moment, and had almost succeeded in waving goodbye to the troublesome box. However, they had not bargained for the suspicion of Peniston and Myers, and had certainly not been prepared for the quickly arranged sale of the premises.

Upon hearing the whole story, the magistrate decided that no proof could be offered as to the parts of Pearson and Wood in this case, and they were allowed to leave the dock, but remained in custody due to the crowds surrounding the courthouse, having followed the progress of this case in the local newspapers over the previous week. The other six participants were ordered to appear before the Yorkshire Assizes:

Wickedly, willingly, and unlawfully conspire, combine, confederate and agree together to disinter a dead body, and afterwards, to wit, in the night of the 2nd of November aforesaid, in pursuance of such conspiracy and agreement, severally enter a church yard, situate at East Ardsley, in the West Riding, and did then and there unlawfully dig up, and disinter from and out of a grave the body of one Robert Hudson and Joseph Longley Fielding, with intent to sell and dispose of the same.

With no real defence to call upon, the men had no choice but to await their fate, which came rather swiftly, as the jury took just two minutes to reach their collective, and unanimous, decision. The gang were told to rise in the dock, as the sentences were handed down one by one.

Teale, who had turned King's Evidence, was discharged (but was left with very little choice but to leave Leeds immediately), and Pickering was acquitted, as the court had heard no evidence to suggest that he was aware of the contents of the box, and had merely allowed it to be stored on his premises (something which the arresting Constable Halton would no doubt have disagreed with). Bradley, Norman and Germaine were each handed down sentences of three months imprisonment, which would be served within the tough regime of Wakefield Prison. Hodgson, who now stood alone in the dock, was sentenced to twelve months imprisonment in the same correctional facility, and was informed in no uncertain terms that his card was now marked.

Very little is known about the future of the convicted men, as none of them appeared before the courts again. Apart from John Hodgson that is, who, unbelievably, left prison the next year only to return to his occupation as a solicitor's clerk! Even more unbelievable is the fact that Hodgson then travelled to Edinburgh, where he practiced as a doctor for a short time (no doubt as a result of his extensive anatomical knowledge), but was eventually removed from his post as it was discovered that his qualifications had been deliberately fabricated.

The ringleader of a criminal gang, who worked in the legal profession whilst disinterring bodies, and eventually became a doctor through no more qualification than his own lies, had been found out. He had finally been disgraced, but not by the heinous acts for which he had been twice imprisoned.

Chapter 5

The Flaxen Haired Boy

'Grief fills the room up of my absent child, lies in his bed, walks up
   and down with me;
Puts on his pretty look, repeats his words, remembers me of his
   gracious parts;
Stuffs out his vacant garments with his form.'

William Shakespeare – King John

Part 1 – The Gamble

To the south of the relatively thriving conurbation of Leeds, a reasonably short twenty-five mile journey through the open fields and small settlements of the west and south Yorkshire countryside lies another town of local significance; one which shared its proud manufacturing industry with its near neighbours to the north and south. Barnsley was the proud provider of much of the coal needed to keep many other local industries operational, and boasted around seventy coalmines within its boundaries, many of which were the epicentre of the small pit villages which sprang up around these valuable natural resources.

First mentioned in the Domesday book of 1086, the town is referred to as *Berneslai* (Barn Field) and was already an inhabited settlement due to the natural resources which were abundant in the area, and would be heavily relied upon centuries later. In addition to their coal-producing prowess, the people of Barnsley were also skilled glass-makers and linen weavers, meaning that during the industrial age, this town, in what is now the county of South Yorkshire, was equally as productive as its industrial neighbours to the south and east. The location of the town was also something of a blessing because, from the seventeenth century, the town became a critical stop-off point between the larger districts of Leeds and Sheffield, ensuring that passing trade was something that could always be relied upon. As such, the town became famous for its hostelries and, whether catering for those travelling through the town or those who had come to seek employment, the inns and guest houses became every bit as important as the local industries.

Although Barnsley did not become a municipal borough until 1869, at the time of our tale the town itself was an ever increasing hive of productivity, providing jobs and housing not only for its residents, but also for the steady influx of travelling workers, who gratefully found work in the many coal mines which surrounded this proud and hard-working town. It is in these cobbled and bustling streets that our incident takes place, and indicates a darker underbelly to this seemingly innocuous and productive town. It all began with an eagle-eyed constable, and a man struggling with a wooden box.

Constable John Gamble was obviously a man who took his profession seriously, as almost a week before our story begins, he had spotted with interest a new couple in town; a couple who seemed to have nothing more to do than spend their days wandering around the busy town centre. In the 1820s, it would have been very unusual for a couple to have no obvious employment and, unless they were of the upper classes, which this couple certainly were not, very few people would have the time available to spend the working week with nothing better to do than loiter in the streets.

It was especially strange as the couple first appeared in late January of 1829, a time of year which is bitterly cold in the northern counties, yet these new arrivals seemed to have no work to attend, and no place to take shelter from the icy winter weather. Consigning their faces to memory, Constable Gamble made the decision to keep a watchful eye on the mysterious couple, although, even in the nineteenth century, it was not the place of a constable to question folk who simply seemed to have an inordinate amount of time on their hands. For the next few days, the couple continued their seemingly pointless walks around the town, and were spotted on several more occasions by the watchful policeman. Yet, they had caused no problems, and had not been of any nuisance, so they were left to their own devices, and their unusual circuitous wandering.

However, on the chilly morning of 2 February, almost a week after their arrival, Constable Gamble noted with interest that the man, now alone, was half-carrying, half-dragging a wooden box through the streets. Keen to find out what he could about this shadowy stranger, Gamble decided to follow until the man reached his destination. Eventually, after a drawn-out struggle with the mysterious box, the man reached the town's Courier Coach Office, and disappeared through the doors with his bulky burden. Moments later, and with a much quicker gait, the man emerged and speedily paced back through the streets before disappearing from sight.

Enthralled by this odd sight, Gamble retraced the man's steps and entered the Courier Office. As a guardian of law and an enlisted constable, it was within his powers to enquire as to the everyday business of such an establishment, and those who used its services. With no reason to question the intentions of Constable Gamble, the employee of the Courier Office, who had been quick to approach the constable and offer assistance, happily dragged the box from behind the counter in order for the diligent policeman to take a closer look. Handling the box, Gamble quickly found it to be more bulky than overly heavy, yet, duty bound by the laws of the land, was at present unable to open the crate, as he had been in possession of not one shred of evidence that anything suspicious was afoot.

There was, however, an address label attached to the box, which was almost indecipherable due to the terrible handwriting in which it had been filled out. Yet, with a few moments of close inspection, it appeared that the address read 'Mary Jones, 1 Princes Street, Edinburgh'.

It was the address that struck a chord in the suspicious mind of Constable Gamble, especially as the famous crimes of Burke and Hare had taken place less than a year before, and was currently the hot topic of every newspaper in the land, as William Burke had been hanged for his crimes just the previous week. A box of this size bound for Edinburgh gave Gamble the shred of suspicion he required in order to make further investigations. Yet, as the law stood, no crime had been committed, therefore he was still unable to open the box for fear of breaking the very laws which he was bound to uphold.

Keen to lay eyes on the mysterious man once more, Constable Gamble hit upon an idea that was to be pivotal in the solving of the puzzle. He asked the Courier employee to contact the man and ask him to return in order to fill out a new address label, as the one currently attached was almost illegible.

Part 2 – A Slow Chase

Had this been a legitimate venture, the man was sure to return and happily fill out another label, keen to avoid delay in the transit of his item. Also, due to the laws that bound the Courier office, the address of the sender could not be divulged without a warrant for arrest. This ingenious ruse would give Gamble a chance to find out more about the man with the terrible handwriting. A covert watch was placed upon the office, and the very next day, with Constable Gamble concealed around the corner furtively watching for his prey, the man appeared. However, instead of merely filling out another address label, he had decided to remove his box from the Courier office altogether.

This very act indicated to Gamble that the man had been suspicious of being called back to the office, and that anyone who would struggle back through the streets with such a bulky item rather than fill out a label, must have very good reason for not wanting to draw attention to the questionable contents. Once again burdened by his cumbersome box, the man was not difficult to follow through the busy streets, and Constable Gamble was hot on his heels. It was not long before the slowest walk the constable had ever taken ended outside a run-of-the-mill travellers' lodging house.

Waiting for man and box to safely disappear into the house, Gamble was determined to find out everything he could about the occupant, before making an approach into what could be a perfectly innocent scenario. Therefore, his first port of call was to the owner of the lodging house. The owner of the premises, Samuel Howarth, kept a cheap, yet respectable lodging house, but also seems to have required very little knowledge as to the business of his guests, as, when questioned by the constable, he could offer nothing but a name in return.

His short-term tenant, who had arrived with his wife and a large box, had given no permanent address, no indication as to his profession, and certainly no clues as to his business in Barnsley. The only other information that could be supplied was that the couple appeared to be fairly local, judging by their strong Yorkshire accents. Satisfied that he had sufficient reason to ask questions of the couple and their business in the town, Gamble asked Samuel Howarth to summon his lodger downstairs, and not to indicate that there was a policeman waiting to question him. The occupant of the upstairs room, already named by Howarth as William Yeardley appeared quickly down the stairs at the request of his temporary landlord, no doubt assuming that the reason for this summons was an innocuous enquiry into a small amount of rent which was still owing.

Yeardley visibly paled upon the site of the constable, and gingerly entered the parlour in the presence of the two men. However, upon questioning, appeared to regain some of his composure, stubbornly refusing to answer any of Gamble's questions unless there was sufficient cause to suspect him of any crime. It was at this point that the subject of the box arose, and the colour once again drained from the ruddy cheeks of William Yeardley. The constable had explained that, due to the events that had been taking place in Edinburgh of late, extra vigilance must be placed upon any items being sent to this particular destination.

Taking in the obvious loss of bravado, which had been so obviously spurred by the mere mention of the box, Gamble asked Yeardley to show him the box, and invited Samuel Howarth to accompany them upstairs, to witness the inspection as a neutral party. By the time the men had reached the top of the stairs, all of the fight and determination seemed to have escaped from the body of William Yeardley, who visibly shook as he opened the door to the room he had rented for the last week.

The woman who had accompanied Yeardley in his furtive wandering of the last few days appeared as soon as the door creaked open, and, like Yeardley, stood silently, drained of all colour as the constable and landlord entered the room and made an instant beeline for the box, which was placed in a corner of the small room. Wasting no time, Gamble asked Yeardley what was in the box, to which he received no reply. Trying his luck with the woman, he again received the same silence in return, and after a moment's consideration, asked Samuel Howarth to bring him a tool with which he could remove the lid. The very instant Howarth had taken his first step towards the door the silence was broken by the terrified Yeardley, who, in a weak and shaking voice, implored of Constable Gamble 'Please...don't open it in here.'

The next few moments passed in silence, as all four occupants of the room stood motionless, frozen like statues in the cold February air. Quietly, Gamble broke the silence, asking in a hushed voice why the box should not be opened, to which Yeardley eventually replied 'Because it contains what you expect to find.'

Once again the silence descended upon the small lodging room, as the gravity of the situation became apparent to all who had witnessed this extraordinary exchange. Again, it was Gamble who regained his composure first, and without raising his voice or creating a scene, placed the couple under arrest.

Part 3 – Uncovering the Cargo

Yeardley and the woman (who, unfortunately, remains unnamed but was posing as the wife of William Yeardley) were soon taken to the nearest police station for further questioning, but during the short journey had regained enough bravado to continue their silent refusal to answer any of the questions posed of them. Meanwhile, with Samuel Howarth still present, a group of constables, including Gamble, began to search the room, and the rest of the premises for any further signs of illegal activity. It would not be long before a telling discovery would be made.

As the scant collection of mismatched furniture in the room was searched, a number of suspicious items were located, having deliberately been hidden from the prying eyes of any unsuspecting visitor. One by one, these were laid upon the bare floorboards, and written down in the notepad of Constable Gamble. Amongst the items found were a shovel with a deliberately shortened handle, screwdrivers, crowbars, and a couple of iron hooks, which were attached to a length of rope. These ominous findings bore all the hallmarks of being the tools carried by those who made their living from a gruesome and distasteful trade.

The tools of the grave robber were easily identifiable. The short handled shovel which could be easily concealed under a long coat, the screwdrivers and crowbars used to prise open the lids of newly buried coffins, and the hooks used to drag their haul back to into the world once again. Handily, for Constable Gamble, the box was not to be opened until later that day, when the couple were hauled before the Barnsley magistrates, in this case being The Reverend Dr Corbett, and Mr Joseph Beckett, who faced a similar wall of silence as the police had experienced while questioning the couple. On

THE

TRIAL
Of the Notorious Highwayman

Richard Turpin,

At *York* Affizes, on the 22d Day of *March*, 1739, before the Hon. Sir WILLIAM CHAPPLE, Knt. Judge of Affize, and one of His Majefty's Juftices of the Court of *King's Bench*.

Taken down in Court by Mr. THOMAS KYLL, Profeffor of Short-Hand.

To which is prefix'd,

An exact Account of the faid *Turpin*, from his firft coming into *Yorkfhire*, to the Time of his being committed Prifoner to *York* Caftle; communicated by Mr. APPLETON of *Beverley*, Clerk of the Peace for the *Eaft-Riding* of the faid County.

With a Copy of a Letter which *Turpin* received form his Father, while under Sentence of Death.

To which is added,

His Behaviour at the Place of Execution, on *Saturday* the 7th of *April*, 1739. Together with the whole Confeffion he made to the Hangman at the Gallows; wherein he acknowledg'd himfelf guilty of the Facts for which he fuffer'd, own'd the Murder of Mr. *Thompfon's* Servant on *Epping-Foreft*, and gave a particular Account of feveral Robberies which he had committed.

The SECOND EDITION.

YORK:

Printed by WARD and CHANDLER Bookfellers, at their Printing-Office in *Coney-Street*; and Sold at their Shop without *Temple-Bar*, *London*; 1739. (Price Sixpence.)

The childhood home of the Turpin family. (*Courtesy of hempstead-essex.org.uk*)

A poster reporting the trial of Dick Turpin. (*Courtesy of Wikimedia Commons*)

JOHN PALMER OTHERWISE
RICHARD TURPIN
THE NOTORIOUS HIGHWAYMAN AND HORSE STEALER
EXECUTED AT TYBURN APRIL 7TH 1739
AND BURIED IN ST GEORGE'S CHURCHYARD

The gravestone of Dick Turpin. (*Photograph by Trevor Stockbridge*)

The Execution of John Bartendale. (*Courtesy of capitalpunishmentuk.org*)

An early dissection performed in Turin, Italy. (*Courtesy of historyofbiologyandmedicine.com*)

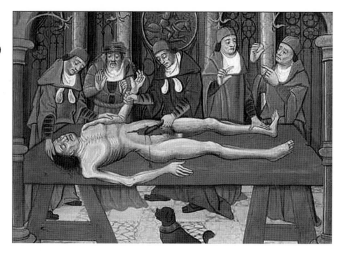

A typical British anatomy theatre. (*Courtesy of mtg-realm. blogspot.com*)

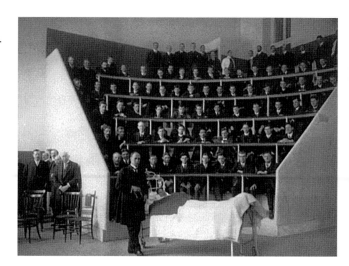

A sketch depicting the execution of William Burke. (*Courtesy of wikipedia.org*)

The skeleton of William Burke. (*Courtesy of murderpedia.org*)

ANATOMY
AND
Physiology.

DR KNOX, F.R.S.E. *(Successor to* DR BARCLAY, *Fellow of the Royal College of Surgeons and Conservator of its Museum,)* will commence his ANNUAL COURSE OF LECTURES ON THE ANATOMY AND PHYSIOLOGY of the Human Body, on Tuesday, the 4th November, at Eleven A. M. His Evening COURSE of LECTURES, on the same Subject, will commence on the 11th November, at Six P. M.

Each of these Courses will as usual comprise a full Demonstration on fresh Anatomical Subjects, of the Structure of the Human Body, and a History of the Uses of its various Parts; and the Organs and Structures generally, will be described with a constant reference to Practical Medicine and Surgery.

FEE for the First Course, £3, 5s.; Second Course, £2, 4s.; Perpetual, £5, 9s.

N. B.—*These Courses of Lectures qualify for Examination before the various Colleges and Boards.*

PRACTICAL ANATOMY
AND
OPERATIVE SURGERY.

DR KNOX'S ROOMS FOR **PRACTICAL ANATOMY** AND **OPERATIVE SURGERY**, will open on Monday, the 6th of October, and continue open until the End of July 1829.

Two DEMONSTRATIONS will be delivered daily to the Gentlemen attending the Rooms for PRACTICAL ANATOMY. These Demonstrations will be arranged so as to comprise complete Courses of the DESCRIPTIVE ANATOMY of the Human Body, with its application to PATHOLOGY and OPERATIVE SURGERY. The Dissections and Operations to be under the immediate superintendance of DR KNOX. Arrangements have been made to secure as usual an ample supply of Anatomical Subjects.

FEE for the First Course, £3, 5s.; Second Course, £2, 4s.; Perpetual, £5, 9s.

N. B.—*An Additional Fee of Three Guineas includes Subjects.*

. *Certificates of Attendance on these Courses qualify for Examination before the Royal Colleges of Surgeons, the Army and Navy Medical Boards, &c.*

EDINBURGH, 10. SURGEONS' SQUARE,
25th September 1828

A pamphlet distributed by the medical school of Dr Knox. (*Courtesy of britishlibrary.typepad.co.uk*)

An artist's representation of the Sheffield School of Anatomy. (*Courtesy of sheffieldtimewalk.wordpress.com*)

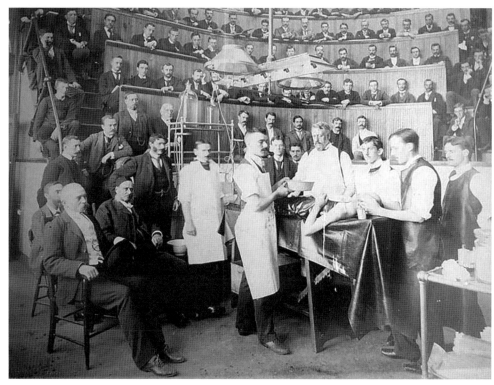

A Victorian anatomy lecture in full swing. (*Courtesy mtg-realm.blogspot.co.uk*)

A portrait of Samuel Roberts, businessman
and social commentator. (*Courtesy of
southyorkshirethroughtime.org.uk*)

A portrait of Dr Corden Thompson, which
still hangs in the Royal Hallamshire hospital.
(*Courtesy of artuk.org*)

A Victorian cartoon depiction of Dr Knox. (*Courtesy of www.spectacularoptical.ca*)

A photograph of modern day Eyre Street, on which none of the historic school buildings now exist. (*Author's Collection*)

A photograph of the Edinburgh School of Medicine as it is today. (*Courtesy of wikipedia.org*)

A photograph of Wortley Cemetery, from where the body of Tom Rothery was taken. (*Courtesy of yorkshiredailyphoto.com*)

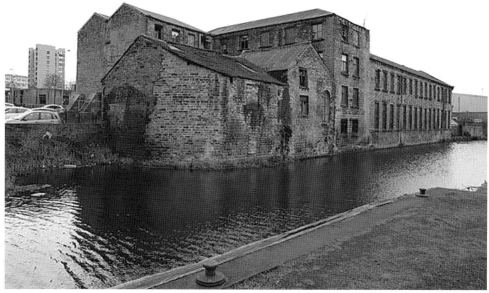

A typical nineteenth century mill on the outskirts of Leeds. (*Courtesy of alamy.com*)

A photograph of the Black Swan, Leyburn.
(*Courtesy of alamy.com*)

A photograph of 'Resurrection Cottage',
taken in the 1930s. (*Courtesy of leodis.net*)

A typical Barnsley
town century street as
would have been seen
in the mid-nineteenth
century. (*Courtesy of
writingfamilyhistory.com*)

A newspaper article reporting on the theft of a body from Attercliffe Cemetery. (*Courtesy of redbubble.com*)

BODY-STEALING,

AT BARNSLEY.

On Tuesday last, February 3rd, 1829, the town of Barnsley was thrown into a state of considerable excitement, by the apprehension of a man and woman charged with the odious offence of body-stealing. The man had for some weeks been noticed walking about the town without any employment or visible means of subsistence, and on this day was observed taking a box to the coach-office, addressed to "Mary Jones, No. 1, Prince's-street, Edinbro'." The constable followed, and suspecting all was not right, insisted on opening the box. The man at first refused to allow him, but finding the officer determined, he said, "Do not open it here; it contains what you expect to find, open it before the Magistrates. He was instantly lodged in "durance vile," and the female who had resided with him as wife or companion, was also taken into custody. The box, on being opened, appeared to be filled with hay, but on removing the latter, a male child, about two years of age, was found at the bottom, without a particle of linen upon it. Its little legs had been contracted so as to prevent the body moving about in the box. It was evident the child had died a natural death, about two or three days before, but nothing transpired to shew the manner in which the body had been obtained. The prisoners were brought before the Rev. Dr. Corbett, and Joseph Beckett, Esq. on Wednesday, and were fully committed to take their trials at the ensuing Pontefract Sessions. On removing the prisoners to their cells, the feelings of the populace were so much excited, that it was with difficulty the officers could protect them from their indignation. No person came forward to identify the child, and it was the opinion of the Magistrates, that it been taken from the neighbourhood of Sheffield. The man declined answering   y questions as to the manner, or from whence he obtained it; but from the evidence of Samuel Howarth, at whose house the prisoner lodged, it is probable that the child came from Sheffield or the neighbourhood, as a man brought the prisoner a basket the night before from this town. A man, who is a weaver in Barnsley, buried a child ten days ago, about four years old; he has examined the grave, but the child is gone: and it is stated by Howarth, that on the night of the funeral, the prisoner and his wife were out till midnight, and the next day a parcel was forwarded to Edinburgh. A regular set of implements was found at the prisoners' lodgings for opening graves and wrenching coffins. They were both committed to take their trials at the Sessions, and an inquest was directed to be held over the child.

The child thus discovered has flaxen coloured hair, with a ringworm on the left side of the head, about the size of half-a-crown, with the hair cut off.—William Yeardley, who is now in custody at Sheffield, states, that he brought the child away from Sheffield in a hamper on Sunday morning the 1st Inst.

We understand that one of the accomplices was apprehended on Friday night last; it appears he left Barnsley about ten days ago, on the coach with a hamper and a box, which are supposed to contain two dead bodies, directed for the said "Mary Jones, of Edinbro'." He returned to Barnsley on Friday afternoon, and enquired for his friend, who was in custody. The person who he enquired of sending for the constable, he was also immediately apprehended. They are supposed to be the same gang that has infested Sheffield and its neighbourhood. We regret to state, that the Church-yards of Barnsley has been plundered of their dead to a great extent.

T. ORTON, PRINTER, SHEFFIELD.

A pre-Second World War photograph of Attercliffe Cemetery. (*Courtesy of picturesheffield.com*)

The rural farming community of Whitkirk. (*Courtesy of www.leodis.net*)

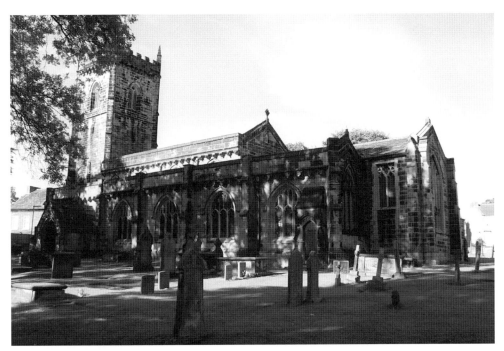

Whitkirk Church. (*Courtesy of leodis.net*)

The interior of the 'White Church'. (*Courtesy of picssr.com*)

Sheffield's grand Cutlers Hall, home to the portraits of some of the city's earliest anatomists and doctors. (*Courtesy of www. storyingsheffield.com*)

Wardsend Cemetery. (*Author's Collection*)

An area of Wardsend Cemetery, close to the 'body pit'. (*Author's Collection*)

An illustration depicting the events of the Wardsend Riot. (*Courtesy of chrishobbs.com*)

Modern day Livesey Street, Sheffield, named after the Reverend who survived the Wardsend scandal. (*Courtesy of wikipedia.org*)

A letter written by Herbert Mayo, in which the early notes of his Anatomy Act were discussed. (*Courtesy of kingscollections.org*)

A sketch of the "London Burkers", a ressurcetion gang who plied their trade in the nation's capital. (*Courtesy of the-east-end.co.uk*)

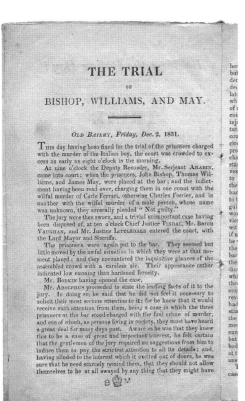

THE TRIAL

OF

BISHOP, WILLIAMS, AND MAY.

OLD BAILEY, Friday, Dec. 2, 1831.

This day having been fixed for the trial of the prisoners charged with the murder of the Italian boy, the court was crowded to excess as early as eight o'clock in the morning.

At nine o'clock the Deputy Recorder, Mr. Serjeant ARABIN, came into court; when the prisoners, John Bishop, Thomas Williams, and James May, were placed at the bar; and the indictment having been read over, charging them in one count with the wilful murder of Carlo Ferrari, otherwise Charles Ferrier, and in another with the wilful murder of a male person, whose name was unknown, they severally pleaded "Not guilty."

The jury were then sworn, and a trivial unimportant case having been disposed of, at ten o'clock Chief Justice TINDAL, Mr. Baron VAUGHAN, and Mr. Justice LITTLEDALE entered the court, with the Lord Mayor and Sheriffs.

The prisoners were again put to the bar. They seemed but little moved by the awful situation in which they were at that moment placed; and they encountered the inquisitive glances of the assembled crowd with a careless air. Their appearance rather indicated low cunning than hardened ferocity.

Mr. BODKIN having opened the case,

Mr. ADOLPHUS proceeded to state the leading facts of it to the jury. In doing so, he said that he did not feel it necessary to solicit their most serious attention to it; for he knew that it would receive such attention from them, being a case in which the three prisoners at the bar stood charged with the foul crime of murder, and one of which, as persons living in society, they must have heard a great deal for many days past. Aware as he was that they knew this to be a case of great and important interest, he felt certain that the gentlemen of the jury required no suggestions from him to induce them to pay the strictest attention to all its details; and, having alluded to the interest which it excited out of doors, he was sure that he need scarcely remind them, that they should not allow themselves to be at all swayed by any thing that they might have

B ⚜ M

A report of the 'Italian Boy' murder, written by a young Charles Dickens. (*Courtesy of bl.uk*)

A watch house, built at High Bradfield, Sheffield, on order to look out for resurrectionists. (*Courtesy of geograph.org.uk*)

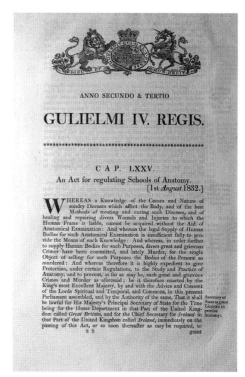

The title page of the 1832 Anatomy Act. (*Courtesy of sciencemuseum.org.uk*)

An example of the use of Mortsafes. (*Courtesy of historyhouse.co.uk*)

A photograph of the church in High Bradfield, Sheffield. (*Courtesy of peakdistrictinformation.com*)

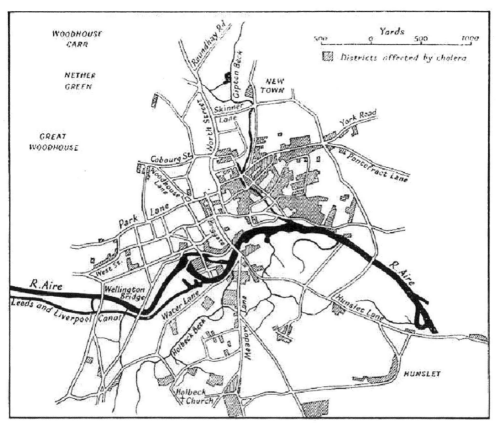

Dr Baker's map of Leeds and the surrounding districts, which depicted the spread of cholera across the city. (*Courtesy of www.researchgate.net*)

A photograph of the abandoned Sheffield Workhouse, close to Kelham Island. (*Courtesy of sheffieldhistory.co.uk*)

The author trying out a grave for size in Whitby.
(*Author's Collection, photograph by Alison Rodgers*)

the orders of the magistrates, and with great care, the box was opened in the courtroom. Its contents hushed those present into a shocked silence, as the lid was slowly and carefully removed. This was a sight that nobody, especially the dumbstruck Yeardley, would have welcomed. On initial inspection, the box appeared to be full of hay, but as the hands of the court assistant delved deeper, it became painfully obvious that that the real cargo lay beneath. Inside, packed tightly to avoid any movement during transit, was the naked body of a small child.

The child, a boy, was so small in fact, that his body was immediately judged to have been around 2 years old, nothing more than a toddler. The hearing was quickly adjourned, and a police surgeon was sent for to perform a more thorough examination. Luckily for the couple who had inhabited the dock, the child was found to have died from natural causes, meaning that a murder charge would not be forthcoming. This was one small mercy for which everybody was thankful, not least William Yeardley and his anonymous accomplice.

However, the two defendants were still in extremely serious trouble. Unwilling to explain from where they had obtained the body, and equally tacit on their reasons for sending the box to Edinburgh, there was no option but for the court to assume that the couple had disinterred the body themselves. William Yeardley and his accomplice were remanded to appear in the court the very next day, in order to answer to the charges against them, and were warned that any further lack of cooperation would see them receiving the maximum sentences which could be handed down by the court.

In the meantime, a poster was drawn up and copies placed around the town. There must have been a grieving parent who had spent the last week mourning at an empty grave, and consequently a detailed description of the unfortunate child was circulated. The boy was described as being 'flaxen-haired, and well nourished and cared for', which could have applied to hundreds of local children, but there was one distinguishing mark that could set this recently deceased boy apart from many others. The child had suffered from ringworm, and as the medication to combat this infection had yet to be invented, displayed a shaved area on the left side of his head in which the circular marks were visible. The shaving of the affected area, at this time, was the only effective remedy to allow the affected skin to heal.

In addition to circulating the posters, it would appear that the police had also been very busy with their enquiries, because by the time Yeardley and his accomplice arrived in the dock the next morning, a full statement had been taken from Samuel Howarth, which was incriminating to say the least. Howarth confirmed that the couple had in fact been his tenants for the last two or three weeks (suggesting that they had originally kept a low profile, as Constable Gamble had only been aware of them for the previous week), and that Yeardley had seemed 'an inoffensive working man.' It was the revelation of some ordinarily innocuous facts however, which were to propel the couple further into serious trouble, and create more questions that the statement was to answer. Apparently, this had not been the only sizeable parcel to have been in their possession during their short tenancy.

The couple had, in fact, been the recipients of two hampers and one large box during the last fortnight, and had received a large basket on Monday 2 February, the very day that Constable Gamble had observed Yeardley struggling with his box on the way to the Courier Office. Despite his apparent lack of interest in his tenants, Howarth was able to offer a valuable piece of information that would give an indication of where the body of the child had been laid to rest. The basket, he revealed, had been sent from Sheffield.

This information was helpful in more than one way. First, it gave the police a starting point from which to locate the family of the poor boy, and second, it laid rest to the rumour that had quickly spread around the town: that the grave robbers had been operating right under their noses. Obviously, the revelation that the child was 'not one of their own' did nothing to quash the sense of outrage and anger that was quickly travelling from house to house in the local area, but did put the minds of recently bereaved Barnsley folk at rest. Overnight, as the story spread, there had indeed been a sense of panic, as these grieving parents from within the town boundaries hurried to the graves of their children, frantically searching for any sign that their final resting place had been disturbed by the abhorrent grave robbers who had appeared in their respectable town. By the next day, when the court proceedings were to continue, the story was the talk of the town. An interesting development had occurred between this hearing and the last however; this time, Yeardley stood in the dock alone, his mysterious accomplice having been released without charge overnight.

Whether the woman was directly involved in the grave-robbing is debatable, as these practices were usually carried out by a lone man, keen not to draw any attention to himself. However, it was common practice for a woman to attend the funeral of an intended target under false pretences. The reason for this would be to find out the age and gender of the deceased, and whether the deceased had succumbed to any infectious diseases, which should be steered well clear of. Also, another duty was to closely observe the burial in order to note whether there were any obstructions, which would make exhumation difficult.

It can be argued that if this was the case, then the woman had not committed a crime, but had been an accessory to a deeply distasteful practice. Also, if Yeardley had claimed to have acted alone, his word would have been accepted, and his partner immediately released.

However, on this occasion, it was decided that the woman had been forced to take part under the influence of Yeardley, a defence that may well have been true, but no corroborating evidence was ever revealed which would have supported the claim, indicating that this was at the discretion of the magistrates.

Part 4 – The Feelings of Mankind

So Yeardley was to face the court alone, and emerged into the dock to the sight of a packed courtroom. The people of Barnsley wanted to see justice done, and they also wanted to catch a glimpse of the kind of man who could perpetrate this kind of sickening crime. Yeardley was described by the local newspapers as:

A decent looking man about 5 feet 4 inches tall. His face is marked with smallpox and he has round features, light sandy hair and whiskers. He has been seen occasionally in Barnsley and Sheffield during the last three years.

As a hush descended over the court and the proceedings began, the case took an unexpected turn as a man, who had only just arrived at the court, was hurried towards the witness box, and began to tell a story which would solve the puzzle of the flaxen-haired boy. The man in the witness box, Mr Flather, was a surgeon who lived and worked in Sheffield. His practice was situated in the Attercliffe area, and he had been called to the bedside of the boy on more than one occasion. His late arrival in court that morning had been due to his attending the police mortuary in order to identify the child as that of the son of a fellow Attercliffe resident, Mr George Bagshawe. The name of the deceased child was, unfortunately, never made public.

Mr Flather went on to describe how he had attended the boy's bedside at the request of George Bagshawe on several occasions during the short illness that was to claim his life, and was also present at the time of the boy's untimely death. The cause of death was an inflammation of the lungs (most probably Pleurisy), which took the life of the unfortunate child within days of displaying the advanced signs of the illness. This illness would also be undetectable to anyone without the aid of a post mortem. He went on to describe how he had read the description in the previous day's *Sheffield Independent*, and had immediately paid a visit to the grieving Mr Bagshawe, who had buried his tiny son less than a week before his cruel exhumation, and was now tending the bedside of his dying wife. The newspaper report appears below:

On Tuesday, the town of Barnsley was thrown into a state of considerable excitement by the apprehension of a man and woman charged with the odious offence of body stealing.

The man had for some weeks been noticed walking about the town without any employment or visible means of substinence, and on this day was observed taking a box to the coach office, addressed to 'Mary Jones, No 1, Princes Street, Edinburgh.'

The constable followed, and suspecting all was not right, insisted on opening the box. The man at first refused to allow him, but finding the officer determined, he said 'Do not open it here; it contains what you expect to find, open it before the Magistrates.'

He was instantly lodged in durance vile, and the female who had resided with him as wife of companion was also taken into custody. The box, on being opened, appeared to be filled with hay, but on removing the latter, a male child, about two years of age, was found at the bottom, without a particle of linen upon it.

Its little legs had been contracted as to prevent the body moving around in the box. It was evident the child had died from a natural death, about two or three days before, but nothing transpired to show the manner in which the body had been obtained.

The prisoners were brought before the Rev Dr Corbett, and Joseph Beckett Esq, on Wednesday, and were fully committed to take their trials at the upcoming Pontefract Sessions. On removing the prisoners to their cells, the feelings of the populace were so much excited, that it was with difficulty that the officers could protect them from their indignation.

No person came forward to identify the child, and it was the opinion of the magistrates, that it had been taken from the neighbourhood of Sheffield. The man declined answering any questions as to the manner, or from whence he obtained it.

But, from the evidence of Samuel Howarth, at whose house the prisoner lodged, it is probable that the child came from Sheffield or the neighbourhood, as a man brought the prisoner a basket the night before from this town.

A regular set of implements was found at the prisoner's lodgings for opening graves and wrenching coffins.

At this point, Mr Bagshawe himself entered the courtroom, just moments after identifying the body of his 4-year-old son (who had been mistaken for a 2-year-old due to the ravages of illness). Silently, he took his seat and, followed by sympathetic glances from the bench and the public, waited for the proceedings to continue. To add to the tragedy, Mr Bagshawe's wife, the boy's mother, had also passed away the previous day, having also been of ill-health and utterly destroyed by the death of her son. On this revelation, the magistrate halted proceedings and asked Yeardley if he had anything to say. 'Nothing' was the cowardly and unabashed answer.

The two men had walked to the Attercliffe cemetery together, and inspected the grave of the child, which they found to be in a state of disarray. The soil was loose and had not been completely filled in, and the items with which the infant had been buried were cruelly strewn across the ground around the grave. Keen to spare Mr Bagshawe from enduring the rest of the proceedings, the magistrate, Dr Corbett, ordered Constable Gamble to accompany the grieving father back to Sheffield, and to arrange for a second, and respectful, burial to be arranged. This was to be at the expense of the county, he confirmed. It does seem fitting that, having prevented the body of the child from being dissected by the hands of the Anatomists, the dutiful Constable Gamble was able to ensure that the child received a proper burial, in which no expense would be spared.

Thus, Mr Bagshawe was escorted home to begin the unenviable task of arranging two funerals, one for his only child, and the other for his wife, who had died without knowing the whereabouts of her recently deceased little boy. Having officially confirmed the identity of the child, and that the body was indeed illegally exhumed from Attercliffe cemetery, all eyes turned to the squirming and wretched William Yeardley, who seemed to have shrunk considerably in size since eyes were last upon him.

One would be forgiven for thinking that this was as bad as things could get for him, but as his temporary landlord, Samuel Howarth, was once again invited to the witness box, another tale of an extremely incriminating nature was revealed, one which would cement his position as a 'professional resurrectionist'.

Howarth recalled that, one on particular evening, the couple had been out until well after midnight. He remembered this day particularly, as it was the day that a neighbour, with whom he was friendly, had held the funeral of their own deceased 4-year-old child. The courtroom predictably exploded into uproar. An account of this incriminating incident also appeared in the *Sheffield Independent* in the following days, and appears below as dictated by the recollections of Samuel Howarth, who had found himself to be the unwittingly pivotal figure of this case.

A man, who is a weaver in Barnsley, buried a child ten days ago, about four years old; he has examined the grave, but the child is gone, and it is stated by Howarth, that on the night of the funeral, the prisoner and his wife were out till midnight, and the next day a parcel was forwarded to Edinburgh.

The chaos in court was further exacerbated by the shocking disclosure that Yeardley had sent a large box to Edinburgh the very next morning, from the very same Courier Office that he had attempted to send the box containing the body of the poor Bagshawe child. So serious were the charges against him that Dr Corbett made the decision to send Yeardley to the Pontefract Assizes to receive his sentence, as the punishments which could be handed out by a magistrate were far more restricted than those which would be imposed by the Assizes. However, Dr Corbett did allow himself the chance to address the room, and in doing so, revealed his own distaste for the work of the resurrectionists, and the medical schools for which they provided their illegally obtained cadavers:

People can talk all they like about the interests of science, and the necessity of diffusing anatomical knowledge, but better that the dissecting rooms are empty than the feelings of mankind should be violated.

Take away that hallowed feeling and veneration for the grave which men entertain, and much will be done to brutalize them.'

Dr Corbett also made reference to the recent death of Mrs Bagshawe, suggesting that Yeardley was *'morally guilty of the crime of murder, since the violence for which he stood charged had led to another premature death.*

The weeks that passed until Yeardley's sentencing in Pontefract were nothing if not eventful, and between his removal from the magistrate's court, under police protection from a barrage of abuse and stone throwing, and appearing in the dock at the Assizes, two more accomplices had been identified and arrested. The arrest of the accomplices was far easier than the covert operation used to track Yeardley. In fact, the two almost succeeded in handing themselves over to the law when they arrived at the house of Samuel Howarth, keen to see a Mr William Yeardley on a matter of urgency.

Seemingly much more alert than previously, Howarth wasted no time in summoning a nearby constable, and the couple were immediately found to have just arrived in Barnsley on a coach from Edinburgh. However, as the two were clearly not of Scottish origin, witnesses were sought who could identify the couple as having made the trip from Barnsley to Edinburgh. Such a witness was quickly found in the form of a coachman who remembered the couple due to the hamper and large box with which they travelled. Peter and Mary Steward, as they were quickly identified, were arrested immediately in connection with the case brought against William Yeardley. The revelation of more resurrectionists within their town caused the people of Barnsley to rise against this deplorable threat, ensuring that vigils were kept in every graveyard and cemetery, and that every suspicious sighting was immediately reported to the police.

The mood was still ugly when the three stood together in the dock at Pontefract Assizes on Friday 1 March, 1829. All three were charged with 'disinterring the body of a child at Attercliffe'. The judge in charge was William Wrightson Esq, and the counsel consisted of Sir Gregory Lewin for the defence, and Mr Maude for the prosecution. Before the proceedings began, Sir Gregory Lewin was allowed to make a speech to the jury, in which he explained the need for dissection in the advance of medical science. However, despite allowing this in the first place, Mr Justice Wrightson soon tired of the lecture and asked the defence counsel to be seated. As in the case of Yeardley's partner, Mrs Steward was adjudged to have been acting under the influence of her husband, and as such was ordered to pay a fine of one penny (which brought jeers and cries of injustice from the public gallery) and was allowed to walk free from court.

Interestingly, it would appear that no attempt had been made to find the unnamed partner of William Yeardley, even though Samuel Howarth had insisted that both parties had been out until after midnight on the night after the local child's funeral. However, Yeardley and Steward were left to face justice for the crimes in which they had been found guilty by the jury. Yet, as no suspicion of either of the men having caused the deaths of these children had ever been raised, the only charge that could be brought against them was that of the desecration of the grave in Attercliffe.

As a human corpse was not seen as a tangible piece of property by the eyes of the law they could not be charged with theft, and they had been very careful to ensure that the objects with which the child had been buried were left by the graveside.

Again, the subject of Mrs Bagshawe's untimely death was raised, and it was with much frustration and fury that Mr Justice Wrightson warned the two men that if he had the power to sentence them for murder, he would certainly have done so. Such a shock, he reasoned, could have easily brought on the death of a woman who was already gravely ill.

Yet, as only the charges of desecration could be upheld, the judge mournfully imposed upon the two prisoners the harshest sentence that was available to him by law in these unusual circumstances: a meagre twelve months of imprisonment for each man. The leniency of the sentence brought widespread condemnation of the laws which bound the judge in this situation, but was no doubt received gratefully by the two men who had deliberately, and willingly, exhumed the body of at least one child for their own financial gain. Such was the tumultuous effect of this case on the people of Barnsley, that concern over the very existence of these resurectionists in the town meant that the local cemeteries and graveyards quickly became full of grieving parents, desperately ensuring that their children had not fallen victim to the business practices of Yeardley and Steward. There were actually accounts of grief-stricken parents removing children from their graves with their own hands, and taking home the tiny corpses in order to keep a watchful vigil over the remains. In response to this, local constables were charged with the duty of attending these houses, and persuading the desperate parents to return their children to the ground whilst accompanied by the policemen, who would then ensure that a watchful eye was kept over the consecrated ground. One can understand the plight of these terrified parents, but eventually, common sense prevailed, and the very real threat of disease and an influx of vermin, which could have been brought on by the presence of the decaying corpses, were dispelled from the modest streets of Barnsley.

No further records exist as to the fate of the two convicted men, but given the leniency of their sentences, it would appear that, in just twelve months, they would have been released back into the streets of Yorkshire, and free to resume their lives amidst the very people whose own lives had been so grievously affected by their immoral actions.

However, if one positive was to arise from this story of grief and sadness, it was to be that the people of Barnsley would no longer let the graves of their loved ones stand unprotected. There would be no more easy pickings for the resurrectionists in this part of the world.

Chapter 6

The Smallest Haul

'Ye have lost a child – nay, she is not lost to you, who is found to Christ; she is not sent away, but only sent before; like unto a star, which going out of our sight, doth not die and vanish, but shineth in another hemisphere.'

Samuel Rutherford – Letter to Lady Kenmure

Part 1 – The White Church

Less than a year before the shocking events which had threatened to stir the town of Barnsley into a wild hysteria, the small suburb of Whitkirk on the eastern side of Leeds had also been touched by its own tale of tragedy and despicable desecration, one which seems all too familiar having heard the sad story of the Bagshawe child.

Situated in the ward of Temple Newsam, Whitkirk remains a relatively quiet and serene corner of West Yorkshire, its streets having changed very little over the last century. Therefore, to discover that the suburb holds a grim tale of body snatching would come as a surprise to most visitors.

The origins of the settlement are largely unknown, but a church in this area is mentioned in the Domesday Book of 1086 and, as St Mary's Church, around which the suburb was created, is the only church of ancient provenance to fulfil this criterion, it is widely assumed that this is the area which was documented. The building that stands now can be traced back to 1185, but as the Domesday Book suggests, there would have been an earlier church on this very site, which would have probably been constructed from stone, as the name of the suburb has evolved from the medieval 'Whitechurche' (White Church). Under its previous nomenclature, Whitkirk is actually mentioned in an ancient charter by Henry de Laci, in which land in the area is given over to the soldiers of the

Knights Templar. Later research of this document showed the agreement to have been made between 1154 and 1156.

As the suburb was built around the ancient church, so is the tale that follows. A tale of sadness and desperation, which took place in the very shadow of the imposing gothic tower, an impressive structure that still adorns the medieval church today.

To set the scene a little more, it is important to take a look at the lives of the Whitkirk inhabitants during the early to mid-nineteenth century. This was a world apart from the busier industrial areas of Sheffield, Barnsley, and central Leeds, and was relatively untouched by the steely fingers of social progression that delved into the neighbouring towns and cities. Much of the area was farmland, which was dutifully toiled by the hands of hard-working families, who lived a modest and self-sufficient lifestyle, tending their crops in order to feed their children, and taking the remainder to the small market which took place under the stern gaze of the church tower.

The market and the church were the hub of the community, places in which the Whitkirk residents could meet and socialise, and were of extreme importance to the suburb, as the farming lifestyles of the population meant that most of their existence was to be solitary and family-orientated, and socialising was something which could only be undertaken when all of the farm work was done. This was a place where everybody knew everybody, but preferred to keep to themselves and concentrate upon their own existence. It would be difficult to find another area so close to the industrial revolution, but as yet untouched by the thirst for progress, which very much defined this era of history.

Religion was almost the only release from this rural life, and the church boasted a healthy congregation each Sunday, priding itself on the morality and modesty of the local residents, and could be forgiven for being unprepared for the despicable act which would shock the citizens of Whitkirk, and induct them into the headlines of the nineteenth century. In many ways, despite the quiet solitude and rural tranquillity, the area had suffered from being left behind by the more developed areas of Yorkshire. Work was limited to the farms, and very little was offered in the way of education, save for the efforts of the church to provide a Sunday school for the local children. Healthcare was also lacking, as poor sanitation, and an almost universal mistrust of doctors, meant that illness and disease were treated by the ineffective combination of poultices and prayer, resulting in a high percentage of infant deaths, all of which could have been avoided by the obtaining of medicine from the nearby towns.

The child mortality rate was also aided by the long and harsh winters which cast their icy shadow over this part of the world every year, leaving the local population open to a wide range of potential illnesses, most of which began with a seasonal chill, and rapidly progressed into much more serious conditions. This annual threat of illness was something of a concern to the local area, but there was one sinister group of people who thrived upon the steady stream of deaths in and around Whitkirk. Even in a place as small and seemingly insignificant as this, the resurrectionists were ready and waiting to unearth their bounty.

Part 2 – An Unexpected Chill

For one family in the area, the festive season of 1828 had brought with it an untimely tragedy; an event which was exacerbated by the unfolding of an unusually changeable winter, which threatened the health and wellbeing of even the strongest members of this rural society, and gave very little concession to the weak.

The early weeks of December 1828 are amongst the mildest ever recorded, with an average temperature of 9 degrees Celsius lulling the county and its trusting residents into the false promise of a very welcome period of winter sunshine. This, however, was not to last. By the end of December, the mercury had dropped to a bone-chilling minus 3 degrees Celsius, and was set to stay this way for the next month. This dramatic drop in temperature had hit the unsuspecting county hard, and as the ice began to spread across the rolling fields and farmland, so did the cold and unforgiving hand of death.

Common colds were widespread, and were quickly followed by a short, but devastating spread of influenza. For many, this was enough to ruin the seasonal festivities, but for the few whose immune systems were not of the highest order, this meant a rapid descent into pneumonia and bronchitis. By the time Christmas Day arrived, most of the Whitkirk residents had taken to their beds, trying in vain to keep out the ever-increasing cold, and firmly closing their doors in the face of the icy winds and stinging sleet which had now replaced the warm embrace of the rare, but dangerously deceptive, winter sunshine.

The church did its best to carry on in the face of these challenges, yet, by the time the usually unmissable Christmas Day sermon arrived, there was only a remarkably small congregation to hear it. No amount of prayer could raise the majority of the town from their sick beds, not even on this, the holiest of religious holidays. It is, therefore, unsurprising that the Christmas of 1828 would be the last for many, especially amongst the elderly and very young who fought the effects of the bitter winter without the assistance of medication, and quickly succumbed to the limitations of their own resistance to the unusually cold weather.

The Yuletide festivities came and went, largely unacknowledged by an increasingly sick population, yet it would not be long before the congregations returned to the church. However, this was not in celebration of the holy season; it was to mourn the passing of many a local resident, and to pray for them as they entered the warmer climes of the afterlife.

Unfortunately, these hastily arranged funerals were not only attended by the grieving members of the local community, they were also attended by at least one person driven by a macabre motive. The resurrectionists stood by the gravesides, and mingled with the mourners, cunningly attempting to calculate the value of the treasure which was buried within. One of the families who gathered their strength to stand beside a grave that had been freshly dug from the icy soil had an especially sad occasion to commemorate. The tiny coffin of their 5-year-old daughter had been lowered into the frozen ground, and with it, a life that had only just begun, and was prematurely ended by a powerful bout of pneumonia.

Hannah Keeson had bravely fought against illness, but her little body had been unable to withstand the ravages of this debilitating condition. Dutifully attending her bedside, the family had been unable to save their daughter, and had no choice but to witness the premature demise of their beloved Hannah. The funeral took place on New Year's Eve, and as 1828 quietly slipped out of sight, so did the small coffin which held the earthly remains of this unfortunate child. This was intended to be Hannah's final resting place; but one particular visitor to Whitkirk had other plans.

Although somewhat cut off from the rest of the world, and ignorant to many of the news stories which were the talk of the town in nearby Leeds and Wakefield, the people of the village had been aware of the threat of the resurrectionists, especially as the local area was remote and unprotected enough to have provided rich pickings for the body snatchers.

It was commonplace for such remote settlements to be targeted, as they were often too far from the view of the police or military to have warranted any concerns about being captured, and as the residents of such places were almost exclusively simple country folk, the burial arrangements were not quite as stringent as those which would be found in larger towns and cities. In light of this threat, the residents of remote areas had employed their own methods in deterring the grave robbers. In the sad case of Hannah Keeson however, the execution of these precautionary measures was sadly lacking, and resulted in a further tragedy for the grieving family. Thomas Keeson, Hannah's father, having just attended the funeral service of his daughter, was determined that such a fate should not befall any member of his family, and as he watched the wooden casket being lowered into the ground, instructed the sexton to take every possible step in order to prevent illegal exhumation.

The most common method of foiling the resurrectionists was to place layers of straw at varying intervals within the grave. This would result in the straw being compacted by the weight of the soil, and therefore render it far more difficult to dig into the ground in order to reach the casket. In a hurry to complete his work and return to a warm fireside however, the sexton failed to perform this duty as requested, and instead, quickly threw a thin layer of straw directly on top of the coffin, before shovelling the frozen earth back into the hole in the ground from whence it had come. Unbeknown to Thomas Keeson, who had left the graveyard after offering his handful of soil to the coffin of his daughter (no doubt too emotional to witness the full proceedings), there was someone by the graveside who took particular interest in the ineffective burial; someone who took particular interest in the contents of the poorly interred casket.

Nightfall would soon spread over the horizon, and the stranger would return to the grave, this time without flowers and condolences, but armed with a lamp, a shovel and a rope. Hannah Keeson would not be resting in her grave by the time the winter sunlight reappeared over the frosty graveyard.

Part 3 –Mistakes and Mistrust

The cold light of morning, which heralded the beginning of a new year, also cast its chilly rays upon a sight which was to throw the entire village into a tumultuous frenzy. A discarded pile of soil stood by the graveside of Hannah Keeson, tacitly announcing that the contents of this resting place were no longer present. The discovery was actually made by Mr Keeson himself, who had made an early visit to the grave of his daughter, despite the bitter cold and freezing rain that descended upon Whitkirk that morning. It is hardly possible to imagine a more upsetting sight for a grieving parent, especially on the morning of New Year's Day.

Keeson wasted no time in waking the sexton from his slumber; hammering upon the door of the rectory with his fists, he demanded that the grave was immediately inspected, and the coffin of his daughter examined to establish whether or not her corpse had been taken. The gravedigger was called for, and arrived soon after Mr Keeson and the sexton had had a better chance to study the condition of the grave. The sexton quickly agreed that this was not how the grave had been left the previous evening, and gave his permission for the gravedigger to begin his sombre duty.

Reaching the coffin would not have taken long, as much of the soil which had been removed was not placed back into the grave, it was left dumped alongside, a sign that the person responsible had either been disturbed whilst trying to exhume the body, or was simply too lazy to refill the grave after he had completed his vile business. It would later prove to be the case that both of these scenarios were true, but the main topic of conversation which accompanied the chilly task of digging down to the coffin was one of angry remonstration from Mr Keeson, who could see quite clearly that his orders had not been carried out as requested. One can imagine that the sexton, who had failed to ensure that layers of straw were used during the burial, was looking on rather sheepishly by this point, well aware that his own reluctance to spend another moment in the cold air had probably aided the miscreant in their criminal efforts.

Upon reaching the thin layer of straw that covered the casket, it was clear to see that this ineffective precaution had simply been pulled aside to allow access to the coffin; a coffin that had not even been closed properly, the loose earth having fallen into the empty wooden box during the meagre attempts to refill the pit. Keeson was inconsolable, and made his anger clear towards the sexton, before desperately calling at every house in the village to see if anyone had witnessed this appalling act of desecration, and could provide any information as to the whereabouts of his recently deceased daughter.

His efforts proved to be fruitless until, that is, a reward was offered for information; a man who was not native to Whitkirk, although a regular visitor, approached Mr Keeson with a wealth of information regarding the crime – a crime which he claimed to have witnessed first-hand. The guilty party was named as Thomas Brown, another non-resident of Whitkirk, but again, a man who was no stranger to the area, having visited on many occasions over the last few months, often taking the time to enjoy a stroll around the graveyard, or to attend the funerals of the recently deceased. Unusually for the area, the local constabulary was brought in immediately upon this revelation. In the majority of circumstances, Whitkirk folk would have attended to their own business, rather than bring in outsiders from Leeds, but this was not everyday business; this was a crime of the most heinous kind.

The accused could not be located in the local area, and it was mentioned by a witness (unnamed) that Thomas Brown had been seen leaving Whitkirk by horse and cart in the early hours of the morning, and appeared to be taking the road which led east from the village, obviously keen to make his getaway before first light. A message to apprehend Brown was put out to all local police forces and was delivered by a horse-riding courier to more distant towns and cities such as Sheffield, Wakefield, Barnsley and Hull. The foresight to include these far reaching places was one that would prove to be invaluable in the hunt for the body of Hannah Keeson.

Brown was apprehended the following day, some fifty-six miles away in Hull, having spent the whole day fleeing the scene of the crime, to what he assumed had been a safe distance. Yet, as he settled down at an inn for warmth and nourishment after his considerable journey, he was immediately dragged from the hostelry by a constable who had received Brown's description just a few hours earlier.

Part 4 – A Future Felon

Brown was roughly escorted to his lodgings, where he had taken the opportunity to stash his possessions before heading for refreshment, and only then was he told of the allegations which had been made against him; allegations which were feebly denied, until the constable ordered that a bulging sack lying on the floor be opened. In a moment of consideration, which would be repeated by a different man a year later during the case of the Bagshawe child in Barnsley, the man was reluctant to reveal his haul to the constable, instead asking to be brought before the magistrate before giving his version of events, largely for his own protection.

His wishes were granted, and both the prisoner and his haul were taken into custody. It would not be long before the truth would be revealed, as he was remanded to appear before local magistrates the very next morning. The sack remained unopened, and would remain this way until it could be brought to the courtroom along with the man who accompanied it. The proceedings, which took place the following morning, were short and perfunctory, despite the gruesome evidence which was presented before the court (although the corpse was not physically presented, it was examined by the police and magistrates before the case was opened) and, with a lack of spectators or reporters, quickly adjourned to be presented at the more prestigious Wakefield courtroom.

It is unusual for a case of such desecration to be held in a largely empty courtroom, but one can imagine that happenings within the small, close-knit, population of Whitkirk were largely unreported at the best of times, let alone in the middle of the harshest winter for a generation. Having given no response to questioning during the hearing, apart from confirming his name and address, Brown was once again remanded into custody and would be held until his appearance before the Wakefield magistrates. Less than three days after his arrest in Hull, Brown found himself in the dock once more, and this time the press had attended the hearing, as had several members of the Keeson family, hoping for justice to be heaped upon the man who had desecrated the grave of their youngest member, and caused untold misery to the grieving family.

Charged with 'disinterring the body of Hannah Keeson, the daughter of Thomas Keeson, from a grave in the churchyard of Whitkirk, and taking it away on the night of 31st December', Brown already had an inkling that the game was up; especially as he saw the man who was about to take to the witness box. The witness informed the court that he had observed the act being carried out as he took 'a midnight stroll' through the courtyard (which is highly implausible given the weather and the late hour), and was able to positively identify Thomas Brown as the culprit of this despicable act. He also claimed to have been familiar with the prisoner, and was claimed to be well aware of his dubious profession, even suggesting that Brown was probably responsible for a number of similar crimes committed in the West Riding of Yorkshire over the previous years. This was immediately dismissed by the magistrates because no proof of these allegations could be offered.

The failure of the sexton to comply with the requests of the family were also discussed, although no criminal charges could be brought against him, as no crime had been committed apart from a lackadaisical attitude to his duties. However, it was suggested that the sexton bear some of the blame for the events that had unfolded that evening. A local newspaper, the *Hull and Eastern Counties Herald*, also confirmed that the burial had been undertaken without care or consideration, and repeated the version of events that had already been given by the father of the deceased child.

Mr Thomas Keeson stated that his daughter was interred in the churchyard at Whitkirk, on Wednesday, the 31st of December, and that he had directed layers of straw to be placed in the grave at different intervals as it was filled up.

The following morning, the grave was found to have been opened, and the body was missing. He said the straw had been put upon the coffin altogether, and not in layers as he had directed.

Originally the sexton had been suspected of deliberately sabotaging the burial, in order to receive a share of the proceeds from the sale of the body; however, no proof existed to confirm or deny this, and the sexton was allowed to leave court with his reputation slightly frayed, but still intact.

When Brown was given the chance to answer the charges against him, he was unwilling to divulge the destination to which he was transporting the body of Hannah Keeson, but did confirm that he had been given an order to obtain a specimen … a small one, either male or female.

Brown's choice of words indicated that the body was indeed intended for a medical school but, having decided to keep his silence on the subject, no further investigation as to the paymaster for whom he was working could be upheld without questioning the heads of every medical school in the land. Despite his reluctance to name his employer, Brown was eager to speak about the man who had appeared in the witness box in order to provide the information, which was now surely to see him imprisoned. To a collective gasp from the court, the man in the dock pointed at the man who had stood in the witness box, and angrily accused him of sharing the very same illegal occupation. The witness smiled wryly as he was once again called to speak before the court, this time to defend his own honour, and waved away all these accusations as being a futile attempt at revenge by the prisoner. The magistrates, Benjamin Dealtry Esq and Daniel Gaskell Esq, agreed, and William Yeardley was allowed to retake his seat in the public gallery.

Brown was sentenced to a month's hard labour, a sentence that bears all of the hallmarks of the lenience often applied in such cases. The court's hands were tied, as in many other cases; the crime was adjudged to have been victimless, as a human corpse was not recognised as a tangible object that could be owned or stolen.

Part 5 – A Broken Bond

The common idiom 'as thick as thieves' certainly does not seem to have been the case in this particular instance, as we know from the previous chapter that the character of William Yeardley was every bit as repugnant, perhaps even more so, than that of Thomas Brown. It would be less than a year before Yeardley would stand in another dock, accused of a crime which bears striking similarities to the disinterment of Hannah Keeson, as he sheepishly stood accused of subjecting the body of the young Bagshawe boy to a similar fate; a fate which, again, was only avoided due to the swift action of the local constabulary. It is reasonable to infer that the two men were well aware of each other, and even saw each other as competition in their macabre occupation. This would certainly explain Yeardley's 'midnight stroll' in the grave yard, and why he was so keen to see his competitor taken out of action by the ensuing court case.

Another remarkable point seems to have been ignored during the questioning of Yeardley by the police after he offered his services as a witness, as he seemed to be almost angry about the shoddy workmanship of his fellow resurrectionist, claiming that such poor technique 'would stop them from doing anything in that way, in the neighbourhood, for a year.' Why this was ignored will always be a mystery, but it is safe to assume that, as no charges were being brought against Yeardley, and he was acting as a helpful witness in the case, the police and magistrates were keen to investigate the incident in question as quickly and as easily as they possibly could.

It is also interesting to note that no information was offered by Yeardley until the £10 reward was mentioned by Thomas Keeson, at which point, Yeardley suddenly remembered that he *had* in fact witnessed the incident, *and* was able to identify Thomas Brown. In a world where honour and basic human values are often cast by the wayside in favour of a quick profit, Yeardley would appear to have surpassed even the most evil of his competitors, as not only had he managed to earn himself a considerable sum of money, he had also managed to be the man who saw to it that his main rival was removed from the competition. This was no doubt a shrewd piece of business, but at least we can satisfy ourselves that this cruel and dishonest man would eventually receive his come-uppance, and would experience the bitter taste of imprisonment and hard labour for himself before the year was out.

Chapter 7

A Riot at the Rectory

'Every man who has in his soul a secret feeling of revolt against any act of the State, of life, or of destiny, is on the verge of riot; and so soon as it appears, he begins to quiver, and to feel himself borne away by the whirlwind.'

Victor Hugo – Les Misérables

Part 1 – A Town within a Town

The view from my home is a rather mixed panorama. In the distance can be seen the rising hills of places such as Loxley, Hathersage and Bradfield, all of them parts of Sheffield which merge seamlessly into the rural majesty of the High Peak.

In the foreground however, lies a busy conurbation. Streets, houses and shops fight for position at either side of the valley, which is itself split into two by a busy main road. The name of this area is known across the globe, but, sadly, not for reasons which bring joy to the citizens of Hillsborough, or the families in many homes across the Pennines. The terrible events which took place in this corner of Sheffield some twenty-seven years ago are never far from the front pages of the tabloids, and the mere mention of Hillsborough often serves to conjure up nothing more than mental images of an event which shocked the nation, and was broadcast live into our homes. These powerful images provide a startling juxtaposition, revealing the bright afternoon sunshine, the flood of coloured scarves and flags and, sadly, the scenes of death and desperation etched upon the faces of those who witnessed first-hand the events of the day which would solemnly inscribe the name of Hillsborough into the history books forever. However, this area of north-west Sheffield is, unfortunately, no stranger to the effects of momentous and unforeseen disaster, and holds an unenviable history of unfortunate incidents, many of which were followed by the unwanted twin visitors of death and grief.

The suburb had grown to a reasonable size by 1779, so reasonably sized in fact, that a name was required for this expanding area. The name of Hillsborough was selected in tribute to the Earl of Hillsborough, who resided in Hillsborough House, County Down, and was formerly the Secretary of State for the Colonies until the outbreak of the American Civil War. The first, and (apart from the events of 1989) probably most notable disaster to befall the suburb came less than a century after its creation, and brought with it an immediate wave of devastation, which was followed by an uncontrollable aftermath of shocking proportion.

The creation of the Dale Dyke Dam had been seen as a forward thinking development for the people of Sheffield, with hundreds of local residents being employed during its creation. Yet, with the technology for assessing the safety of such a large project being many years in the future, the physics of undertaking such a large piece of construction were based largely on guesswork and estimation. On the night of 11 March 1864, the time had come for the reservoir to be filled for the first time, and it was with pride that the chief engineers allowed the water to begin flowing into the vast concrete basin, which, unfortunately, was not strong enough to keep its contents from escaping as rapidly as it was filled.

During that fateful night, a crack opened up in the embankment, which spread as quickly as the water could travel into the dam and, in just a few short hours, a catastrophic event was to befall the residents of the local area. Assisted by a strong gale, the destruction of the newly built dam continued throughout the night, and before any warning could be given, an estimated 700 million gallons of water swept down the Loxley Valley, before reaching the densely populated areas of Hillsborough and Malin Bridge.

The devastation of such a powerful flow of flood water can only be imagined, but when one considers that the water was to eventually reach Rotherham, which joins Sheffield some eight miles on the opposite side of the city, it is easy to see how such an event could be so devastating to those affected. Hillsborough itself had largely borne the brunt of the disaster, with most homes and businesses destroyed by the floods, and forty-two residents killed directly by the flood, or by the collapse of buildings that accompanied the water along its unstoppable march to freedom. As ever, the collective will of the Sheffield citizens was unbreakable, and the clean-up operation began the very next morning, but the disaster had not quite finished with the city yet, and the aftermath of the floods was almost as devastating as the previous night's deadly events.

The irreplaceable comfort of sanitation had been all but wiped out by the flood water, and amidst the scenes of destruction and heartbreak came vermin and disease, which were eventually to claim more lives as typhoid began to spread across the area. The graves of the victims and various monuments commemorating these events can be found in the local area today, dotted amongst the churchyards and cemeteries of this corner of the city. However, it is in one of these very graveyards that just two years earlier, in 1864, a shocking event had taken place, an event that had already shocked the residents of Hillsborough.

The great leaps made in the scientific pursuit of medical knowledge (which would now, ironically, be required more than ever in the aftermath of the floods) had long since been eyed with mistrust, and actual fear by the simple, God-fearing Yorkshire folk of the local areas.

The catalyst of this wave of distrust had peaked some thirty years earlier, during a notable incident in which the city's new medical school had been burned to the ground by suspicious locals, who had been fearful of the desecration of human corpses within the walls of the school (see chapter 2).

The suspicions of the Sheffield public had never been laid fully to rest, and even in 1862, almost three decades later, the hushed tales of unspeakable acts and gossip of distasteful practices still passed through the local communities like wildfire, leading to an event which was to shatter the relative peace of Hillsborough.

Part 2 – An Opportunistic Investment

Wardsend Cemetery was a fairly new addition to the Owlerton area of Hillsborough in 1862, having only been consecrated by the Archbishop of York, Thomas Musgrave some three years previously. Before this consecration, the land had been an unused and uninhabited area of woodland. The cemetery still exists to this day, and is unique in being the only cemetery in the country to have had a functional railway line running through it – something that may have caused the railway labourers a little concern during maintenance work on the tracks!

The land was actually purchased in 1857 by Reverend John Livesey of nearby St Philip's church, a piece of business made necessary by the overuse of the graveyard on the church grounds. At the time of the purchase, Reverend Livesey had been commended by the local community for his investment, but all of that was to change in the following years. The land had cost Reverend Livesey almost £3,000, a huge amount of money in the 1850s, and it was noted in the records of the time that most of the funds were donated by the Reverend himself, with the aid of small church and council grants. The subsequent building of a small, yet beautifully designed, chapel and a house to accommodate the sexton of the church, Isaac Howard, only served to add greater costs to this development, and left a small shadow of suspicion in the minds of those who doubted the genuine charitable nature of Reverend Livesey. The first burial to take place at Wardsend was of a local child, 2-year-old Ann Marie Marsden, who, as tradition dictates, became the symbolic 'Guardian of the Cemetery'. One can only imagine that this was scant consolation to the parents of the child, but was something of an honour nonetheless.

Over the next few years, the unfortunate population of the cemetery began to grow, and this consecrated ground became a popular place to lay loved ones to rest owing to its picturesque setting, and the relative ease in securing a plot. The most noteworthy burial at Wardsend was that of George Lambert, a soldier who had been awarded the Victoria Cross for his bravery and distinguished conduct during the Indian Mutiny of 1857. However, it is sad to note that Lambert died not in battle, but of illness, aged just 37, hundreds of miles from his birthplace in County Armargh. The ever-benevolent Sheffielders accepted this brave young man as one of their own, and, as his death had occurred within the city, took it upon themselves to raise funds for a fitting burial, and lined the streets in their hundreds to witness the funeral procession. The graveyard has always been closely associated with the nearby Hillsborough Barracks, and acts as the resting place for many a fallen soldier. As the barracks had been home to a number of regiments, it would seem that this association provided the cemetery with plenty of business over its many years of operation.

By 1862, the outskirts of the five-acre grounds had also been used to build a handful of houses, something that may have been in Reverend Livesey's original plans, as a way of recouping a percentage of his vast expenditure. These humble abodes were rented out to local workers, and the arrangement seemed to be mutually beneficial to both church and community. The people of the area were provided with much needed housing, and the church, via the collection of rents, was able to rely on a steady income in order to bolster its depleted coffers. Unfortunately, it was this misguided practice of mixing business and religion which sparked a series of distasteful events which would tarnish the extemporary reputation of Wardsend cemetery, and the good Reverend who had, up until now, been seen as shining example of Christian virtue by the majority of his parishioners.

Part 3 – The Catalyst

The catalyst that caused the truth to be unearthed was something of an innocuous incident, in which a former resident of one of the houses situated within the church's land, a Mr Robert Dixon, became involved in an argument with the sexton, Isaac Howard, the man who had previously been charged with collecting his rent. The two had formerly been friends, and, although the disagreement is believed to be of a trivial nature, it has never been proven that it had anything to do with the former relationship between the men as tenant and rent collector.

Clearly holding a grudge after their recent quarrel, and with an extraordinary, yet unproven, tale to tell, the former resident, Robert Dixon, a quarry labourer by trade, decided to approach his employer, Mr Oxspring, a man with good standing in the local community, and shared with him a macabre story of dubious goings-on which had occurred during his residence within the cemetery grounds. Dixon claimed to have been disturbed by a foul smell during his residence, and felt it his duty as a tenant to investigate the source. This had taken place in March of the previous year, and Dixon believed that it was the gradual warming of the weather that had served to exacerbate the pungent odour.

The origin of the unpleasant aroma was discovered to be in a room above the stable, from which the smell leaked more strongly than anywhere else within the grounds. Covering his face to the foul and sickening air, Dixon claimed to have made a discovery that would rock the formerly tranquil and leafy idyll of Wardsend cemetery.

Having identified the source of the problem, Dixon began to make a hole in the floorboards of the upstairs room, as the stable itself was permanently under lock and key and, having succeeded in pushing through a knot in one of the boards with his pocket knife, knelt to peer inside the closely guarded stable. The sight that allegedly greeted Dixon was even more unpleasant than the almighty stench. He claimed that through the hole he had created in the floorboard, he was confronted with an image that would haunt him for the rest of his days.

The story is now taken up by *The Times* of 9 June 1862, in which Dixon's subsequent testimony was printed in all its gory details:

Robert Dixon. – 'I am a labourer in the service of Mr Oxspring, of Wardsend. I know Isaac Howard, the sexton of this cemetery. I agreed with him to go and live in his house in the graveyard. I cannot tell exactly the day of the month, but it was sometime in March last.

Shortly after I had gone there I observed a curious smell in the room above the stable. I thrust some knots out of the deal boards, and looked down into the stable. We had then been there two or three weeks. I saw about 20 coffins – some of persons about 15 and 16 and 10 years old – others were those of stillborn children.

None of them appeared to be the coffins of grown-up persons. I had seen Howard lock and unlock this door, and knew he had the key. The coffins were not covered over with anything, and were lying on the ground, piled in heaps on the top of each other. I saw some broken-up coffins piled in a corner by themselves – the wood appeared to be new.

Those pieces are there now. The day I flitted (last Monday) I and several other men saw in the stone shelf near the house four or five sides and lids of coffins. They were in a dark corner of the shed.

I lifted up the lid of one coffin, in the shed, about six weeks ago. The night following the body had been removed from the coffin, but the coffin remained in the shed. I lifted the lid with my toe, and saw the face of the body. It looked very fresh, as though it had been buried a week or two. It looked like the face of a boy about 15 years of age.

I looked at the coffin the same night, after Howard had set off to Sheffield. Had seen him go. He put two corpses into a box. One appeared to be 10, and the other 15. I saw the same coffin empty in the shed the same night. I afterwards went and looked through the holes in the floor.

I came home earlier than usual. I thought he looked very queer and 'sheepish' in my eye. I had had suspicion of him before. I saw him go in and out of the house and go up the burial-ground. I went upstairs and looked through the holes in the floor, and waited until he came back into the stable.

He appeared to be cutting off the leg of a child about 10 years old. The child lay on two planks and he had a carving knife in his hand. I saw him put the bodies into a box. He put the lid on and went outside the door, and came in again immediately.

He put the box on a barrow, and went to the river side. I saw him put two bodies into the box. The stable is not so large as the room overhead, in which I was. The holes were large enough to admit my finger. There is a small slide window in the top of the stable, with only four or five panes in it. I once found the stable door unlocked, about three weeks ago, and saw about 20 coffins and 24 coffin plates.

I took the plates away and gave them to Mr Oxspring. They are the same he has given to the chief constable. I had previously told Mr Oxspring, and was acting under his advice in what I did. The sexton asked me to take the house. We have had a quarrel, but were good friends before I left the house.

I met him on the burying-ground. I asked him if I could cultivate a bit of ground, and he consented on condition that the ground should be given up if there were any Catholic funerals. He spoke very angrily to my wife about the place, and I wished to see him, and told him he had better take those bodies out of the coach house before he said anything to my wife.

We parted good friends. I have once been in trouble for stealing some corn, four years ago, at Ellaby-hall (sic). That is the only thing of the kind I have ever been in to my knowledge. I had married just before.'

Having told his chilling tale of gruesome practices within the consecrated grounds, it was then revealed that the wife of Mr Dixon, Bethiah, was also

party to allegedly strange goings on which disturbed their relatively short
tenure as residents at Wardsend.

*We went to live in that the house in the graveyard on the 24th of March.
When we first went I noticed a peculiar smell in the room over the stable,
and it got worse. I spoke to the sexton about the smell, and he said he would
remove it – it would go away.*

*I have seen the porter from the Medical School go up the burial-ground.
He came more than once. I first saw him there on the Thursday in the second
week we went to live there, which would be on the 3rd of April.*

*I told the sexton that the man had been to see him, and the man came
again on the Friday morning, but he did not see the sexton. I told the sexton
again, and he said he had seen him, but he (the porter) had no money for
him, and until he got some money he (Howard) should not let anything else
go.*

*I have seen a man named 'John,' who assisted Howard, remove coffins
from graves and put them in the open shed. The sexton afterwards put them
into the stable. The men opened the graves and removed the coffins from
them.*

*These graves were not distinguished by mounds of earth. Judging from the
size of the coffins which 'John' and Howard removed, I should say that they
were those of children about ten or 12.*

*About a fortnight ago I saw Howard remove some coffins from the stable
into the large pit. He took some in the day time, and towards evening he got
the assistance of another man. I saw a man named Coldwell helping him.*

*I never saw any other person at the pit than Howard and the two men
assisting him. I never saw any funerals performed at that pit – not at that
particular place. I have never seen any service performed at that pit. There
was one small place open, so as they could slide a coffin into it, but it could
be made larger.*

*The pit was covered with planks and a thin layer of earth. There were
planks placed against the hole when they were not using it. I remember the
holes being made in the floor of the room over the stable. I looked down and
saw coffins there. I have looked on several occasions when my husband has
been away.*

This incredible tale of unspeakable acts is, indeed, a vivid and detailed account of the alleged events of the previous spring. However, one must question why such a lurid story was only divulged to anyone over a year later. It would make sense that the argument between Dixon and Howard had provided the spark that lit the fire underneath this macabre secret, yet, in those days of religious duty, and especially with money to be made from the newspapers, it does seem odd that the tale only came to light after an innocuous disagreement.

However, the events that were to follow the revelation of these secrets to the upstanding Mr Oxspring were nothing short of explosive, as it would seem that Oxspring wasted no time in sharing this tale with anyone who had the fortitude and stomach to hear it.

Part 4 – Wildfire

It appears that the tale shared on that fateful afternoon soon began to make its rounds in the local inns and taverns, as well as over the garden fences of the residents who lived within the immediate vicinity of the cemetery because, by that evening, the locals had stirred themselves into quite an agitated state.

There had long been clandestine whisperings in regards to the practices which took place behind the cemetery gates of Wardsend, but most had dismissed these as being the kind of tales which often do the rounds in close-knit communities; especially those which lie in close proximity to the resting places of the dead. One such rumour was that, of the four clock faces that adorned the tower of St Philip's Church, one was never lit; this, it was surmised, was to allow the graverobbers to work in darkness. Whether this was true or not, it does seem interesting that the same observation had been made by many local residents before the Dixon's grim discovery. It could also, of course, have been a case of a faulty clock. One would imagine that, if such nefarious activities were taking place, the church would have done everything possible to avoid drawing attention to the area, rather than displaying a clock face notable for its lack of illumination.

Stories of dim lights being observed in the dead of night, accompanied by whispering, and suspicious sounds of creaking and digging, also spread in the wake of the rumours but, without knowing the ins and outs of working practices within the cemetery, it is impossible to endorse these tales with any kind of credence. However, these powerful rumours did exist, and the discovery of the macabre scene in the cemetery's stables brought the horror stories hurtling back to the public imagination – and added some extra potency to the increasing ire of the whispering masses.

By nightfall, a large crowd had descended upon the cemetery, possibly buoyed by alcohol and the kind of exaggeration that often accompanies such rumours (although, it must be said that the details of the story themselves, if true, required absolutely no exaggeration). Akin to an epic scene from any good Hammer Horror film, an angry and frightened mob determinedly made their way towards the cemetery, holding aloft flaming torches and gas lamps because, given the nature of the story they had been party to, nobody wanted to enter this place in the pitch of darkness. Eyes were peeled for any sign of movement in the darkness, and all ears were pricked in anticipation of the sounds of footsteps or whispering. However, one would imagine that, with a loud and illuminated mob approaching from the distance, anyone present in the cemetery at this time would have made a quick retreat towards safety. The mob was made up of a wide cross-section of the Hillsborough population. Men, women, and even children, jostled to be at the head of the procession, all of them determined to find out the hotly-anticipated truth for themselves.

Mingled within this approaching crowd were relatives of loved ones who had been buried in graves within the grounds, desperately hoping the stories to be untrue, but prepared, nonetheless, to find out for themselves whether their loved ones had been laid to rest as their religion dictated. These grieving members of the mob searched frantically in the dim light for the graves of their relatives and friends, and having pre-emptively armed themselves with picks and shovels, began to strike at the ground in which the bodies were said to have been buried. The remainder of the crowd, intent on retribution and with a sense of religious duty, broke off from their frantically digging cohorts, and stalked the grounds with an unparalleled sense of anger and outrage, their eyes darting in the dark for any sign of the custodians of the cemetery.

It was, reportedly, only a short time before one of the groups who had armed themselves with picks and shovels cried out into the night, urging anyone within earshot to join them with their torches and lanterns to inspect a suspicious discovery. A pit had been uncovered, which allegedly contained the decayed bodies and broken-up coffins of a number of corpses. However, this in itself was not enough evidence to determine whether foul deeds had been committed. The pit itself could have been nothing more than a communal pauper's grave.

Even in their frenzied state, the mob were aware that proof of wrongdoing was required, and it would not be long before the discoveries of that fateful night fell into place like some ghastly jigsaw displaying a scene of darkness and dismay. The full account of these allegedly shocking findings was later reported in *The Times* in all of its gaudy glory, with absolutely no concession being made for any readers of a weak or nervous disposition.

As the news of the discoveries spread through the town, the parents and relatives of many of the persons buried in the ground proceeded to the place, and numbers of them began excavating the graves in order to satisfy themselves that the remains had not been tampered with.

In several cases no trace of the coffins could be found, and this, of course, greatly increased the excitement. The most revolting discovery of all, however, was made in an unused part of the cemetery grounds, where was found a large hole, roughly covered with earth and planks, and containing about 20 coffins, and a box in which were the remains of a man who had been dissected at the Sheffield Medical School.

It was found that underneath the coffins was a mass of human remains several feet in thickness, which were alleged to have been accumulated by the throwing of dissected bodies into the hole without coffins, and the emptying of bodies from coffins removed from graves in the cemetery.

A number of coffins, and 24 coffin plates, removed from coffins which had been placed in the ground within the last three years, were found in the stable. The examinations of the place which were made in the course of the week disclosed such a state of things that the Bench were loudly called upon to interfere to punish the offenders and secure the future protection of the public.

Mr Jackson, Chief Constable, said he had to apply to the magistrates to aid him in the investigation of the circumstances which had notoriously occurred at the Wardsend burial-ground and at the sexton's house; he stated that on going to the cemetery he found in the side of the hill a large hole.

It had no appearance of having been arched, but there were boards driven in at the side to support it. The hole had been covered with planks and earth, but this, the people had removed. He saw a square box containing what evidently were the remains of a man, and also a number of coffins, 20 inches broad and 15 or 18 inches deep.

He had the square box removed to the cemetery stable. Having got another box made sufficiently large to hold the one taken from the hole, he had it and the body put into this new box and brought to the police-officers here.

It was a deal box, about 3 feet 6 inches long 20 inches broad and 15 or 18 inches deep. The box did not appear to have been buried. The body had evidently been dissected, the flesh having been removed from the bones.

The crowd were now more agitated than ever, and descended upon the coach house belonging to the newly maligned sexton, Isaac Howard. Howard, perhaps having been forewarned, had fled the area, leaving his home undefended in the face of this volatile mob.

It was at this point that the crowd, perhaps spurred on by the disappointment of finding nobody at home to answer their allegations, began to turn increasingly furious, and from this point onwards, this fateful night was to become a permanent scar upon the former beauty and tranquillity of the cemetery. As with all riots, it takes a single spark to ignite the touch paper of civil unrest, and on this occasion, the first stone aimed at the window of the coach house provided the catalyst for a torrent of wanton vandalism, which was to spiral more and more out of control as the night progressed. Stones became rocks, and threats became reality as, buoyed by the occasion, the usually mild-mannered people of Hillsborough gave in to the anger, which they had previously managed to contain. This was truly to become a night of infamy.

Within minutes, all of the windows had been shattered, and the doors of the coach house kicked into splinters from their sturdy frames by the muddy boots of the local residents who had marched to the cemetery intent on seeking some kind of retribution with the unspeakable acts of which they had been recently informed. As the doors gave up their integrity, the mob swarmed into the premises, taking the opportunity to destroy everything in their wake. Furniture was dragged from the house and reduced to firewood by hundreds of brutal shovel blows and pickaxe swings.

Shamefully, it was revealed in the later testimony that an occupant of the house was still at home. The unfortunate Mrs Howard had been cowering in fright at the violent invasion of her home, and was dragged in a state of terror from the premises by the jeering and vicious mob. Terrified beyond control, and reeling from the attack on her home, Mrs Howard pleaded with the attackers for her life; a plea that was accepted in the light of reason, as even an angry mob could see when a faithful wife had been abandoned by her cowardly husband.

However, the house itself was not to be spared, and as the unfortunate Mrs Howard tearfully looked on, her home was thoroughly and repeatedly vandalised by the picks and hammers which had now been called upon to replace the rocks and stones used against the windows and walls of the rapidly crumbling abode. Before long, the coach house was entirely destroyed, the quaint and solid structure bore no resemblance to its former self, and instead, it stood a hollow corpse, surrounded by the splinters of the once fine furniture that had cosily resided within its walls. The orgy of destruction was then capped by an incongruous *coup de grâce*, as the remains of the house, which had stubbornly remained standing in the face of such an onslaught, were set alight, the flames casting an eerie glow upon the twisted and tormented faces of those who had angrily descended upon the building.

Exhausted from their exploits, and in need of a moment's contemplation, a temporary hush descended over the crowd, as they began to sit upon the consecrated ground and watch as the fire consumed the focal point of their collective rage. It was several hours before the crowd dispersed, exhaustedly returning to their homes, muddy and smoke-stained, yet with a sense of satisfaction that some kind of primitive justice had been delivered that night.

Again, we turn to the pages of *The Times* for a description of the events.

It will be remembered that on Tuesday night a large crowd of people, exasperated beyond all control by the horrible disclosures that had been made of the manner in which human remains were desecrated, broke into the sexton's house and set it on fire.

Mrs. Howard narrowly escaped with her life. Damage to the extent of £500 was done at that house and at the cemetery. The mob searched for the sexton, but could not find him, fortunately for him.

Part 5 – Awkward Questions

It is worth noting at this point that the owner of the grounds, and the man ultimately responsible for its day-to-day operation was left in peace. Reverend Livesey, in fact, remained at the church rectory and was undisturbed by the events of the evening. Perhaps it was with a sense of religious trust that the rioters simply believed that such a community leader could not have knowingly allowed such things to take place upon the consecrated land, which had so recently been purchased for the benefit of the local community? This however, is uncertain, as although the Reverend himself, and his home, were left undamaged by the incident, the chapel within the cemetery had also been badly ransacked and vandalised, something which would dispel any notion of a sense of collective religious conscience within the rioters.

Having been left to face the music by his sexton, Reverend Livesey was to spend the next week undergoing rigorous questioning from the fledgling Sheffield Police Force, and was forced by the laws of the land to divulge any business practices in which he was involved. Unfortunately for Livesey, the nature of some of his dealings were seen as dubious by the investigating officers, and as a result, he was required to appear before the magistrates to provide answers to these unusual allegations.

Isaac Howard had successfully fled into the night, leaving behind his faithful wife to face the baying mob who descended upon their home, so intent on capturing the man whom they believed was responsible for such sickening acts of desecration and ungodliness. Howard could not hide forever though, and after a week spent flitting between Bakewell and Derby, where friends had provided much needed refuge, he made his way back to South Yorkshire, fearful of the consequences, but determined to clear his name.

He was apprehended at the Red Lion Pub, in the Masborough area of nearby Rotherham, where he had arrived by train the previous day. Howard had actually contacted the investigating officers to inform them of his imminent homecoming, but after deviating from his promise of meeting the detectives in Sheffield, was eventually collected from the tavern by two officers. Detectives Airey and Brayshaw took the short train journey to apprehend their suspect, and only when they met Howard in person, did they realise that the sexton believed them to be escorting him for his own personal protection. The sexton earnestly believed *himself* to be the victim in all of this. It was to his great surprise that Howard learned that he was to be brought before magistrates, and that a warrant for his arrest had been issued to Airey and Brayshaw before their short train journey to Rotherham. It would seem that certain matters had been uncovered during the questioning of Reverend Livesey, which were of considerable interest to the police.

In a strange order of events, Howard first appeared before the magistrates to petition damages for the destruction of his home, and to request compensation from the city for damage that had been caused on the night of 3 June. It would seem that, in the light of such explosive events, the magistrates were keen to remove any red tape from the case at the earliest opportunity. However, at the end of these civil proceedings, Detective Brayshaw quickly approached the bench, and, to gasps from those present, applied to remand Howard into police custody for questioning in relation to a charge of having illegally removed the remains of a child from their rightful resting place.

Howard was visibly shocked and confused by this turn of events, and asked for the charges against him to be clarified. However, the disgraced sexton was denied this explanation, and was immediately refused bail by the magistrate, Mr A Smith, from which point, he was entirely at the disposal of the police. He did not have long to wait for his explanation, as the very next day, Howard was brought, once again, before the magistrate, and this time was party to an incendiary statement made by a local resident in relation to the alleged desecration of a child's grave.

Part 6 – A Clergyman in Court

The following testimony from Mrs Harriet Shearman is taken verbatim from the court reports, which appeared in the *Sheffield Independent* the following morning.

I am the wife of William Shearman, miller, Philadelphia Mill-yard. My little boy, Edward Charles, died about eight months ago; he was then two years and one month old. He was interred at the St. Phillip's ground on the 23rd of September last.

The grave was made on the left-hand side over the hill, on the lower side from the railway. I paid 1-s. for the fees of burial to the sexton, Isaac Howard. I only saw a little bit of earth put on the coffin at the time. He told me I could have a family grave by paying a further sum of 22s within the year.

In consequence of what I heard I went up to the ground on Wednesday. I went to a large pit there was in the cemetery, and saw some coffins there. Some of them had the lid off, and in one of these I recognized the features of my own child.

I got it taken out of the pit with the coffin, and caused it to be taken home to my own house. When I got it home I examined the coffin, and found it was the same wood. I found the piece of a 'bump' sheet which I had placed beneath the head of the child.

I am quite sure from the features, and from this sheet, that it was my child.

When I left the grave at the funeral the sexton was there. He had the care of the grave at that time. We have another child there, or it should be there. The hole where the body was found is about 200 yards from the grave where we left my child.

I looked into the grave, but cannot recollect whether the soil was firm or soft, as if it had been previously dug. There were funerals going on in the ground at the same time. I don't know who performed the service.

My first child was interred in the ground three years ago. This child was not buried in the same grave, because we had not bought the ground. We have not looked for the coffin of the first child.

This shocking and tragic statement did nothing to repair the rapidly plummeting reputation of the erstwhile sexton, and brought cries of revulsion and anger from those who had successfully squeezed their way into the heaving courtroom. Further cries were heard as the prosecuting solicitor addressed the bench, and stated that he was in possession of similar statement from a number of women, but they were not present in the court that day. The case was adjourned to appear before Leeds Assizes at the end of the following week, during which time Mr Howard would continue to be held in police custody. It would not be long before the full and gruesome details of the events at Wardsend cemetery would be revealed. Overjoyed that there appeared to be movement in the proceedings, the public did find themselves in the dark as to another factor of the case. Reverend Livesey had still not been released from custody. It was with a sense of shock that they learned that the good Reverend was to join his colleague before the Assizes the following week, and that due to his stature in the local community, his arraignment had been held privately before the magistrates.

The next week passed in a flurry of rumour and supposition, and as the majority of the local community would not be attending the proceedings in Leeds, all they could do was wait until the newspaper reports were released on the following day. During this brief hiatus in the proceedings, a public meeting was held at the Peacock Inn, local to the church and its extended grounds, in which a large group of Hillsborough residents made their negative feelings known as to the character of the man they had so revered as a servant of God within their community.

The next evening, a larger meeting was hastily arranged at Sheffield's Temperance Hall, in which a crowd of over 3,000 people demanded that Livesey be suspended until the outcome of the trial. However, the representatives of the Church of England who had attended announced that they would reserve their opinions unless guilt could be proven. Those waiting with baited breath for the revelations to be made public were certainly not disappointed by the outcome. Neither of the men was to walk free from the court room that day; and a story that would shock the entire nation was revealed piece by piece in front of the jostling throng of reporters, who clambered for a view of the defendants.

It would seem that the charges brought against Reverend Livesey were indeed in relation to some of his more unusual business arrangements, and that he was to answer to an accusation of making false entries in the Register of Burials. The charges stemmed from an arrangement that Livesey had with the much-mistrusted Sheffield Medical School, in which he would inter the bodies of the corpses that had been dissected by the anatomists, conveniently leaving out the details of how they came to be in the possession of the cemetery, and also omitting to reveal the payments received from the school for his services.

This was confirmed by a man named Moses Walton, who worked as a porter at the medical school, and was a regular visitor to the Wardsend cemetery. His surprisingly honest statement appeared in the court transcript as follows:

'I have been in my present employment nearly 12 months. Two months after I came I had to see Isaac Howard, the sexton of St. Philip's, to make arrangements for the interment of a dissected body.

I arranged with him to take if from the Medical-hall to the cemetery. On the 10th of March last I took the body of Joseph Greatorex from the workhouse to the Medical-hall. I saw that body at the Medical-hall many times subsequently. I had taken it there by the order of Mr Barber, the secretary.

The body remained at the Medical School until the 12th of April. It was put in a box by me and Howard. Afterwards Howard took the box away on a wheelbarrow. I had seen Howard at Sheffield, and given him instructions with regard to that body, on the 3rd of April.

I told him to fetch it from the Medical-hall and take it to St. Philip's Cemetery. He was to take it there for burial. It was not removed on the 3rd of April. I did not see him again until the 12th, when he fetched the body away. I paid him 5s when he fetched the body.'

The witness also proved that it was the custom for the Medical School to pay Howard 13s for the interment of each body, that sum including the usual burial fees and the price of a coffin or shell.

So, it would appear that the much-maligned Isaac Howard, was, in fact, working under the close direction of Reverend Livesey, who was providing an unusual service to the community in disposing of the bodies which were no longer required by the anatomists of the medical school.

This was further confirmed by the next witness, who appeared in the box to agree that the statement of the porter was indeed correct. This time, the witness was of even greater standing in the community, being as he was, a surgeon of considerable reputation. Again, the following statement from Mr Joseph Barber is taken verbatim from the court proceedings.

I am a surgeon in Sheffield and member of the Royal College of Surgeons. I hold the Secretary of State's licence to practice anatomy at the Medical School in Surrey Street. I produce the original book in which I make entries of bodies received from the Sheffield Workhouse.

I received the last on the 10th of March. It was that of Joseph Greatorex. That body remained at the Medical School several weeks. After sending Walton to Mr Livesey I received the certificate produced.

I have been in the habit of making general arrangements for the interment of these bodies, and always received a certificate of their interment, signed by Mr Livesey.

They have always been in the form of the one I have produced. I have paid the fees for the interment of those bodies. I paid those fees to Howard, the sexton. I paid him for the interment 13s, and he had 5s before, which made 18s.

Although the revelations which had so far been uncovered were mainly in regards to dubious and inappropriate financial dealings, the next statement, from Mr Joseph Couldwell, who had worked alongside Isaac Howard at the cemetery, was a more revealing insight into the lack of pastoral care given to the bodies received at the cemetery.

His testimony was damning and descriptive, yet was just a mild introduction to the gruesome tales that would be heard in the packed court room on that shocking and unforgettably eventful day.

I know Isaac Howard and worked under him at St. Philip's burial ground. I know a stable upon the burial ground. Howard kept the key. I moved a box out of the stable into the coach-house, by Howard's directions, a month ago last Saturday.

I afterwards moved it from the coach-house to the pit, which was in another part of the ground. The box was in the coach-house eight days. I removed it on the Sunday night. There were the remains of a man in the box when I removed it the last time. I did not know that the first time. I saw a thigh-bone.

The body was in a bad state of decomposition. Howard took it from me at the pit. The pit or catacomb was a big hole covered with beams and planks, upon which there was a covering of earth. Howard put the box into the hole.

A month ago I took some coffins to the same hole, and the box was placed upon them. It had never been interred anywhere. There was no clergyman present when the box was taken to the hole.

The Burial Service was not read over the remains in the box. I saw the box and remains at the Town-hall a fortnight ago last Friday, and am sure they are the same I saw in the hole.

This lack of care and the absence of any religious ceremony were confirmed by another witness, Jonathon Sutcliffe, who elicited shrieks of disgust from the public gallery when he informed the judge that he 'had seen Howard turn human remains out of a box, and shovel them into a pit.'

The mood of disgust was not helped by the statement of Detective Brayshaw, the policeman who had apprehended Howard in Rotherham, and had required the sexton to accompany him to the cemetery to investigate the allegations. One can only imagine the outrage of those present in court, and their reaction to the following statement. However, it is easy to imagine that there were some queasy folk listening to the proceedings on that unforgettable day.

Part 7 – The Gory Details

Detective Brayshaw's statement was, thankfully, the last of the proceedings, and certainly did not help to repair the reputation of the two formerly upstanding pillars of the community who now sat grey-faced and pensive in the dock. Ever dutiful, and with copious handwritten notes in his official notebook to refer to, Brayshaw was able to accurately, and minutely, describe the details of the events which had unfolded following the night of unexpected violence and rage which had proceeded his arrival at the cemetery.

> *On Saturday evening, I and Inspector Crofts went to the Wardsend Cemetery between 7 and 8 o'clock. I took Howard, the sexton, there. At my request he opened the coach house door. He took the keys out of his pocket to unlock it.*
>
> *In the coach-house I saw a square box. I took off the lid, which was loose on. I saw portions of a human being in the box – I believe the trunk. I then proceeded to the pit.*
>
> *By my orders the pit was opened, and I saw very many coffins in it. The soil of the pit was dug into by a young man at my request, and after a few shovelfuls of earth, he dug up parts of a human being – the legs and thighs in a complete state of putrefaction.*
>
> *I went to the cemetery again on Tuesday, and there saw the same box with the remains of a body in the pit. I feel sure it was the same box and contents. The remains had the appearance of not having been interred.*
>
> *The same box and remains were afterwards brought to the Town Hall.*

The defendants were asked if they had anything to say in response to the evidence they had heard against them. Isaac Howard simply shook his head, and Reverend Livesey, with an air of resigned panache addressed the judge and said 'I reserve my defence. I leave the case entirely in the hands of council.' This did little to sway the public towards any sympathy for the two defendants, as the tales of discarded corpses and butchered flesh burned into their collective conscience, and the lack of any remorse from the instigators merely served to add insult to injury.

An eye witness statement was then introduced by the prosecution, describing the terrible scene which had been discovered by one of the more educated rioters, who had taken to Wardsend cemetery on that night in order to see the evidence of these horrific allegations for himself. His statement largely mirrors that of Detective Brayshaw, but served to raise the level of disgust of the public gallery, revealing as it did, more gory and unthinkable details of the practices which had been hidden within the grounds of the cemetery.

The number of coffins (found in the communal pit) was nearly twenty, some being evidently those of stillborn or very small children, but others those of older children and a few adults. Some of the coffins contained no corpses, but there were portions of flesh, which appeared to have been trodden under foot, presenting a very sickening sight.

I also saw one body which had been cut to pieces and packed in a square box. There was no doubt that this was one of the dissected bodies previously alluded to. The sight appeared to move deeply the feelings of the persons who were present.

At about half past nine, they began to vent their rage by throwing stones at the window of the house which Dixon had occupied. It should be here stated that Dixon had left the house a short time before, and it was now furnished for the use of the incumbent resident.

Having learned that the Sexton lived at Burrowlees, nearly a mile distant, the mob next proceeded to his house. It is stated that an intimation had reached Howard of what was likely to happen, and that he had left his house to avoid an encounter with the mob.

However this may be, Howard had gone out, leaving his wife alone in the house, and she had fastened the doors and shutters.

Despite the tawdry facts of the case, and the gruesome testimonies that had tested the digestive fortitude of many of those present, there was one factor that cast a huge doubt over the whole situation. Had any crime actually been committed?

Part 8 – Remembrance and Recrimination

It was without doubt that the facts of the case were inflammatory and indicated towards a complete lack of religious compassion or a moral sense of duty, but a corpse, in the legal sense, did not exist as a tangible human being, or even as an object. Therefore, the mercy of the two men in the dock was entirely in the hands of the judge, and his perception of the charges. There was an unproved inkling that Howard had been involved in more serious incidents, which suggested that as well as receiving cadavers from the medical school, he had also been supplying them for dissection, an allegation backed up by the testimony regarding the child whose body had been removed from the grave, and unceremoniously buried in the pit.

This at least gave grounds to charge Isaac Howard with disinterring a body (which *was* actually a crime, although one which was exceedingly difficult to prove had been done with malice aforethought) and left just the question of how to deal with the unusual financial arrangement of the Reverend. After much discussion at the bench, it was eventually decided that falsifying a burial record was an act of fraud, and as such, punishment could be handed down to the man who had overseen the horrors of Wardsend, but, until this point, was guilty of nothing more than a distasteful business arrangement.

Reverend John Livesey was found guilty of making a false entry of burial, based on the empty grave of young James Greatorex, and of creating a false death certificate in relation to the same boy. However, as no further fraud could be proven, his punishment was to be a nominal three weeks imprisonment. His sexton, Isaac Howard was slightly deeper in the hot water, as he was actually identified as having been present at, and participating in, the unsavoury practices at Wardsend. However, his sentence was almost as lenient as that of his employer, as he was handed a punishment of three months imprisonment. It should also be noted that Howard was awarded £200 on his release from prison, as compensation for the destruction of his home. This was easily enough money to ensure that he and his wife could move away from Sheffield, and begin a new life away from the gory goings-on in this particular corner of Hillsborough.

Reverend Livesey had no such plans, and immediately returned to St Philip's church upon his release from prison. The church council had decided in his absence that, due to his huge financial contribution in obtaining the land in the first place, he was entitled to recoup his money, albeit in a macabre fashion, and that no serious crime had been committed.

Surprisingly, it would appear that the Reverend was soon accepted back into the community, and was to soon regain the trust of his parishioners, who were satisfied that he had meant no malice in his actions, and were more than willing to attend his well-regarded sermons. This was largely due to another development in the case, in which Isaac Howard had publically admitted full responsibility for the scandal, meaning that Reverend Livesey was eventually pardoned, although rumours did exist that Howard had left the area with a considerable sum of money with which to start his new life.

The following excerpt is taken from a piece which appeared in the *Sheffield Independent* shortly before the death of Reverend Livesey in 1870, in which the author 'Criticus' pays tribute to the character of the man, and alludes to his past controversies.

There was the choir at the top of the centre aisle, and there were the choristers, ten nice little boys in white surplices, five on each side, and six men, all in surplices.

The singing and chanting were unquestionably good. There was nothing higgity-jiggity about the tunes, anthems, or music. The congregation did not join in the response very extensively.

The service was conducted by Mr. Livesey, whose style of reading is easy, fluent, rather rapid and somewhat familiar. In the pulpit he wore his academic gown, having never worn his surplice when preaching since 1847, when his wardens presented him with an address, thanking him for giving it up.

The text was four words, 'Enoch walked with God,' and the sermon occupied sixteen minutes. In private life Mr. Livesey is a very worthy and estimable character.

He is genial, benevolent and kind hearted. He has a just and enlightened apprehension as to what is due to his position as incumbent or vicar of St. Philip's, and has on several occasions sacrificed himself to uphold great principles.

Like Job, Mr. Livesey has had to 'endure affliction,' and, as in the case of that patriarch, his 'latter end' yields a redundant return of peace and plenty.

Sitting under his own vine and fig tree in the pleasant retreat of Wadsley Grove, none daring to make him afraid, he rejoices in the esteem of his friends and parishioners.

Such was the re-emergence of the formerly disgraced Reverend that a road was named in his honour. Livesey Street now runs across the back of Owlerton racetrack, and, ironically, is also the home to the Hillsborough campus of Sheffield College. It is due to this remarkable turnaround in public opinion that the events of the Wardsend cemetery riot have been largely forgotten. The sentences were quickly and quietly served, and life, for those who had been involved, went on without hindrance.

However, the incidents of 1862 have not been forgotten entirely, and a memorial stone situated in a walled garden in Hillsborough Park, which was crafted deliberately to the dimensions of a child's coffin, bears the inscription:

> *To the affectionate remembrance of Frank Bacon,*
> *Who departed this life April 2nd 1854, aged three years.*
> *Also Louis Bacon aged four months*
> *Buried in Wardsend Cemetery April 12th 1858.*
> *And was one of the many found in 1862.*
> *Who had been so ruthlessly disinterred.*

It is easy to forget the impact that these tasteless and immoral exhumations would have had on the families of the deceased, especially those who would go to their own graves never being entirely sure that the resting place of their child had been left unmolested. As such, it has been possible, from obtaining the original news reports, to provide a list of those children whose coffin plates were found, unscrewed and cast aside in order to provide a safe guarantee of anonymity, not for the children, but for the men who had dragged them from what should have been their last resting place.

The list is copied below, and details only the names that could be made out from their coffin plates. Of the twenty-four plates found secreted within the foetid stable at Wardsend, only fifteen could be deciphered, leaving nine children to leave this life unnamed. The dates found on the plates indicate that this practice had been taking place for a number of years, with the earliest being from 1857, some five years before Robert Dixon had made his macabre discovery within the cemetery outbuildings.

Those whose lives could be recorded were:

Sarah Ellen Frost, died 24 April 24 1858, aged 1 year
Richard Henry Parker, died 23 May 1858, aged 9 months
Charles Hinchcliffe, died 6May 1858, aged 2 years and 11 months

Mary Roberts, died 28 April 1858, aged 2 years
Emma Willett, died 28 December 1858, aged 1 year and 1 month
William Henry Cornall, died 23 May 1858, aged 3 years
John Beatson, died 29 July 1858, aged 4 years
John Lilly, died 14 March 1858, aged 4 months
Anna Shearer, died 26 February 1858, aged 47 years
Louis Bacon, died 9 April 1858, aged 4 months
Sarah Jane Davis, died 16 October 1857, aged 5 years
H.B. Waite, died 15 August 1858, aged 2 years and 4 months
Charles Wood, died 22 March 1858, aged 10 months
Charles Marshall, died 12 May 1858, aged 5 years
Sarah Ellen Durden, died 7 March 1858, aged 7 months

Chapter 8

The Death of the Resurrection

'Laws are like cobwebs, which may catch small flies, but let wasps and
hornets break through.'
  Jonathan Swift – A Critical Essay upon the Faculties of the Mind

Part 1 – The Beginning of the End

In 1828, a report had been compiled by eminent physician, and member
of the Royal Society of Surgeons, Herbert Mayo, which urged the
government to take direct and urgent action in regards to the widespread
problem of body snatching, which, by this time, had become far too regular
an occurrence across the nation to ignore.

However, as with many well thought out reports, the government, in their
wisdom, did decide to ignore the warnings set out by Mayo, and instead
decided to combat the issue by merely denying the size of the problem, and
choosing to bury their collective heads deeper into the safety of the sand.

The medical schools were still getting through a huge amount of corpses,
and as the only legal route to obtaining these was the donation of executed
criminal cadavers, it was clear to all involved that the sums did not add up.
Every student of anatomy was expected to have dissected three corpses by
the time they graduated university, yet the number of executed criminals
would not have even provided for one corpse per student; something which
the government did their best to staunchly ignore. Of course, the regular
flow of bodies arrived courtesy of the resurrection men, and without these
clandestine business transactions, the medical world would have ground to
a halt, and medicine as we know it could have been very different, even in
today's modern age.

The arrangement, which prevailed until decisive action was finally taken,
seemed to benefit most parties. The schools got their corpses, the resurrection

men got their money, and the government was spared from taking any stance on an issue that promised to be as thorny as an acre of rosebushes. Yet, not everybody benefitted from this arrangement; the families and loved ones of the cruelly disinterred bodies certainly did not benefit, nor did the legal profession, who were expected to act against crimes of this kind, but did so with one hand tied behind their back, as the punishments available were so meagre in comparison to the gravity of the crimes.

The famous case of Burke and Hare (see Chapter 1) had recently brought the subject of body snatching to the forefront of national news, and the British people had started to become wise to the ruse of the resurrectionists. Yet, it would be another four years before the cobwebs were blown from Mayo's report. Mayo was not deterred by the failure to pass the act that he had so meticulously compiled, and spent the next few years perfecting his work. Yet, it was to be circumstance rather than common sense that eventually paved the way for Mayo's Anatomy Act. By coincidence, Mayo had actually been involved in the case which would eventually prove to be the catalyst for the passing of his Anatomy Act; something which, no doubt, caused him to add several caveats to the work which he had already complied.

The incident in question, which was to became famous as the murder of 'the Italian Boy' took place in 1831, just two years after the publically celebrated execution of William Burke, and was almost as explosive as the trial of the two Irishmen, perhaps even more so as it occurred in London, right beneath the noses of the government. This fascinating story began when the body of a 14-year-old boy appeared before the porter of the King's College School of Anatomy. It had been delivered to the secluded rear entrance of the premises by two local men, both of whom were well known to the porter and could be relied upon to provide corpses of excellent quality for the students to dissect.

The two men were John Bishop and James May (known locally as 'Black Eyed Jack', or 'Jack Stirabout'), members of a notorious gang of London resurrectionists, which also included Thomas Williams and Michael Shields. All in all, these were not the kind of characters one would like to do business with under normal circumstances. Known locally as the 'London Burkers' (having taken the name of William Burke, the forerunner of their lucrative business empire), it was suspected that these four men had been involved in hundreds, if not thousands, of grave robberies over the last two years. Unbeknown to the porter, the body was actually in remarkable condition, so remarkable in fact, that Guy's Hospital, another of London's famous medical establishments, had already turned the men and their top quality wares away, most likely because the freshness and condition of the corpse was a little too good to be true. However, the porter at King's College accepted the cadaver, which was transported into the building following a heated row in regards to payment. Bishop and May were adamant that the body was worth twelve guineas, but left with only nine, possibly due to the fact that they had already been turned away by the rival establishment.

Yet, when inspecting the body, the more educated and skilled eye of Richard Partridge, a lecturer in Anatomy, found things to be amiss with this new specimen. The body was too clean and too fresh to have been buried, which could mean only one thing: that the body had been obtained by extremely dubious means. Consulting his superior, who just happened to be Herbert Mayo, Partridge voiced his concerns, and asked Mayo for his opinion. The respected professor quickly concurred with his younger colleague, and sent him to the nearby police station at Covent Garden, instructing him to return with a constable. The findings were immediately relayed to the police, who had very little cause to doubt the opinion of two such educated men, and a warrant was obtained for the arrest of the two 'Burkers', who were quickly rounded up along with their colleague, Thomas Williams. All three men were found at the same house, number 3 Nova Scotia Garden, which was officially the residence of John Bishop, but had been used for the last year as a regular meeting place for the gang, and were immediately placed into police custody until the post mortem of the body, and the subsequent inquest had been completed. The public inquest was held on 8 November 1831, and wasted no time in recording a verdict of 'wilful murder against a person unknown'. It was also suggested that the involvement of the gang was very likely, and that the unidentified boy had been murdered by one, or more, of the men who now languished in gaol.

The Nova Scotia Garden premises were thoroughly searched by Superintendent Joseph Sadler Thomas, who, after scouring every inch of the premises, found several items of clothing in an outside privy, and many more submerged in a well at the foot of the garden. This suggested that the mysterious boy was not the only person to meet his end at this address. In an unusual move, the police then opened the house for public viewing (charging visitors for the privilege of gawping at such a macabre venue), during which time almost every piece of furniture, and any object not nailed down, were taken as souvenirs by the constant flow of paying guests.

By the time the case was heard in the Old Bailey, the boy had been identified as Carlo Ferrari, a teenager who had emigrated from Piedmont, Italy, along with his family the previous year. This led to the case being hailed as 'the murder of the Italian boy' on the front pages of local and national newspapers. Due to a lack of evidence against him, Michael Shields was freed from gaol, but was warned in no uncertain terms that his life would be in danger of he were to stay in London. The other three men were to stand in the dock together, and were found guilty of involvement in the murder of Carlo Ferrari. Whilst awaiting their fate, as sentencing had been adjourned to allow for further investigation, Bishop and Williams found the burden of guilt too heavy to bear, and sent for the prison officials in order to make a full and frank confession to the murder, and also to exonerate James May, who the pair claimed to have had no involvement in the matter, apart from helping to carry the body to King's College.

The two prisoners, however, denied that the body was that of Carlo Ferrari, and claimed that the corpse was in fact the remains of a Lincolnshire farmhand, whom they had encountered as he left the cattle market at Smithfield. To this day, the true identity of the body has yet to be discovered, although most believe that Carlo Ferrari was, in fact, the unfortunate victim. The boy had been taken into the Nova Scotia Garden house with the promise of lodgings, and had then been drugged with a mixture of alcohol (probably rum) and laudanum. While the boy slipped into unconsciousness, the two gang members went to a local inn, and returned later that evening to check that their victim was in a pliable state. Finding the boy to be in a comatose condition, they then attached a cord around the boy's ankles, before throwing him head first into the well. They then went back to the inn (the Feathers in Shoreditch) and returned home later to drag the lifeless body from the well. They then stripped the body and placed it into a large sack, ready to be transported to whichever medical school would offer the highest reward and so ended the life of a boy who could have been either an Italian immigrant, or a Lincolnshire farmhand.

To the amazement of the officials who had gathered to hear the confession, the men appeared to have been familiar with the old adage 'one might as well be hung for a sheep as for a lamb' as after a short conversation in private they agreed to admit to two more murders, in addition to countless acts of body snatching from the local graveyards. They had, they admitted, employed the same method in the murder of a homeless woman, Frances Pigburn, who had been sleeping rough, and gratefully accepted the offer of a hot meal and lodging for the night. The body of Frances Pigburn had then been sold to King's College for eight guineas. The ruse was also used on another young boy named Cunningham, who was found sleeping rough in the Shoreditch area. His body too fetched the sum of eight guineas, seemingly the price of a life to the members of the 'London Burkers'.

May was released, but received the same warning as Michael Shields, and spared no time in escaping the city, no doubt thankful that that his two colleagues had at least held onto some slim shred of decency during their incarceration. Bishop and Williams were sentenced to death, and hanged at Newgate Gaol and, just like in the case of William Burke, who had been such an inspiration to them, their bodies were immediately placed on a cart and taken to the dissection tables of the London colleges.

Part 2 – The Anatomy Act, 1832

The case of the 'London Burkers', along with that of their idols, Burke and Hare, had finally woken the government into taking action against the ever-increasing threat of the resurrectionists. The works of Herbert Mayo were reintroduced in parliament, and this time, were taken much more seriously than on the previous occasion. Mayo could now add his own personal experience to the many pages of compelling evidence, and as such, found himself welcomed with open arms in the seat of British; unlike the events of two years previously, when he had been largely ignored, and sporadically ridiculed.

The main articles of the act are printed below, and are very useful in highlighting the rigid procedure that would be introduced with regard to the obtaining of corpses for dissection. No longer would the medical schools be allowed to turn a blind eye to the questionable source of their valued specimens. Never satisfied with using one word where several would suffice, the government published the below and provided a copy to every Member of Parliament, after which, the Act was passed through the House of Commons, and subsequently, through the House of Lords.

Mayo had finally made his mark, and the wordy, yet powerful, document, which appears below, is testament to his hard work and unshakeable professionalism. The dead would be allowed to rest in peace (unless their demise fulfilled very strict criteria).

1. *Immediately on the passing of this act, or so soon thereafter as may be required, to grant a licence to practise anatomy to any fellow or member of any college of physicians or surgeons, or to any graduate or licentiate in medicine, or to any person lawfully qualified to practise medicine in any part of the united kingdom, or to any professor or teacher of anatomy, medicine, or surgery, or to any student attending any school of anatomy, on application from such party for -such purpose, countersigned by two of his majesty s justices of the peace acting for the county, city," borough, or place wherein such party resides, certifying that, to then knowledge or belief, such party so applying is about to carry on the practice of anatomy.*

2. *It shall be lawful for his majesty's said principal secretary of state or chief secretary, as the case may be, immediately on the passing of this act, or as soon thereafter as may be necessary, to appoint respectively not fewer than three persons to be inspectors of places where anatomy is carried on, and at any time after such first appointment to appoint, if they shall see fit, one or more other person or persons to be an inspector or inspectors as aforesaid ; and every such inspector shall continue in office for one year, or until he be removed by the said secretary of state or chief secretary, as the case may be, or until some other person shall be appointed in his place ; and as often as any inspector appointed as aforesaid shall die, or shall be removed from his said office, or shall refuse or become unable to act, it shall be lawful for the said secretary of state or chief secretary, as the case may be, to appoint another person to be inspector in his room.*

3. It shall be lawful for the said secretary of state or chief secretary, as the case may be, to direct what district of town or country, or of both, and what places where anatomy is carried on, situate within such district, every such inspector shall be appointed to superintend, and in what manner every such inspector shall transact the duties of his office.

4. Every inspector to be appointed by virtue of this act shall make a quarterly return to the said secretary of state or chief secretary, as the case may be, of every deceased person's body that during the preceding quarter has been removed for anatomical examination to every separate place in his district where anatomy is carried on, distinguishing the sex, and, as far as is known at the time, the name and age of each person whose body was so removed as aforesaid.

5. It shall be lawful for every such inspector to visit and inspect, at any time, any place within his district, notice of which place has been given, as is hereinafter directed, that it is intended there to practise anatomy.

6. It shall be lawful for his majesty to grant to every such inspector such an annual salary, not exceeding one hundred pounds, for his trouble, and to allow such a sum of money for the expenses, as may appear reasonable; such salaries and allowances to be charged on the consolidated fund of the united kingdom, and an annual return of all such salaries and allowances shall be made to parliament.

7. It shall be lawful for any executor or other party having lawful possession of the body of any deceased person.

8. If any person either in writing at any time during his life, or case of persons verbally in the presence of two or more witnesses during the illness whereof he died, shall direct that his body after death be examined anatomically, or shall nominate any party by this act authorized to examine bodies anatomically' to make such examination, and if, before the burial of the body of such person, such direction or nomination shall be made known to the party having lawful possession of the d.ead body, then such last-mentioned party shall direct such examination to be made, and in case of any such nomination as aforesaid, shall request and permit any party so authorized and nominated as aforesaid to make such examination, unless the deceased person's surviving husband or wife, or nearest known relative, or any one or more of such person's

nearest known relatives, being of kin in the same degree, shall require
the body to be interred without such examination.

9. *Provided always, that in no case shall the body of any person be removed*
   for anatomical examination from any place where such person may
   have died, until after forty-eight hours from the time of such person's
   decease, nor until after twenty-four hours' notice, to be reckoned from
   the time of such decease, to the inspector of the district, of the intended
   removal of the body', or, if no such inspector have been appointed, to
   some physician, surgeon, or apothecary residing at or near the place
   of death, nor unless a certificate stating in what manner such person
   came by his death shall previously to the removal of the body have
   been signed by the physician, surgeon, or apothecary who attended
   such person during the illness whereof he died, or if no such medical
   man attended such person during such illness, then by' some physician,
   surgeon, or apothecary' who shall be called in after the death of such
   person to view his body', and who shall state the manner or cause of
   death according to the best of his knowledge and belief, but who shall
   not be concerned in examining the body after removal ; and that in case
   of such removal, such certificate shall be delivered, together with the
   body, to the party receiving the same for anatomical examination.

10. *It shall be lawful for any member or fellow of any college of physicians*
    or surgeons, or any graduate or licentiate in medicine, or any person
    lawfully qualified to practise medicine in any part of the united
    kingdom, or any professor, teacher, or student of anatomy, medicine,
    or surgery, having a licence from his majesty's principal secretary of
    state or chief secretary as aforesaid, to receive or possess for anatomical
    examination, or to examine anatomically, the body of any person
    deceased, if permitted or directed so to do by a party who had at the
    time of giving such permission or direction lawful possession of the body,
    and who had power, in pursuance of the provisions of this act. to permit
    or cause the body to be so examined, and provided such certificate as
    aforesaid were delivered by such party together with the body.

11. *Every party so receiving a body for anatomical examination after*
    removal shall demand and receive, together with the body, a certificate as
    aforesaid, and shall, within twenty-four hours next after such removal,

transmit to the inspector of the district such certificate, and also a return stating at what day and hour and from whom the body was received, the date and place of death, the sex, and (as far as is known at the time) the Christian and surname, age, and last place of abode of such person, or, if no such inspector have been appointed, to some physician, surgeon, or apothecary residing at or near the place to which the body is removed, and shall enter or cause to be entered the aforesaid particulars relating thereto, and a copy of the certificate lie received therewith, in a book to be kept by him for that purpose, and shall produce such book whenever required so to do by any inspector so appointed as aforesaid.

12. It shall not be lawful for any party to carry on or teach anatomy at any place, or at any place to receive or possess for anatomical examination, or examine anatomically, any deceased person's body after removal of the same, unless such party, or the owner or occupier of such place, or some party by this act authorised to examine bodies anatomically, shall at least one week before the first receipt or possession of a body for such purpose at such place, have given notice to the said secretary of state or chief secretary, as the case may be, of the place where it is intended to practise anatomy.

13. Repealed

14. No member or fellow of any college of physicians or surgeons, nor any graduate or licentiate in medicine, nor any person lawfully qualified to practise medicine in any part of the united kingdom, nor any professor, teacher, or student of anatomy, medicine, or surgery, having a licence from his majesty's principal secretary of state or chief secretary as aforesaid, shall be liable to any prosecution, penalty, forfeiture, or punishment for receiving or 'Having in his possession for anatomical examination, or for examining anatomically any dead human body, according to the provisions of this act.

15. Nothing in this act contained shall be construed to extend to or to prohibit any post-mortem examination of any human body required or directed to be made by any competent legal authority.

16. Repealed

17. Repealed

18. *Any person offending against the provisions of this act in England or Ireland shall be deemed and taken to be guilty of a misdemeanour, and, being duly convicted thereof, shall be punished by imprisonment for a term not exceeding three months, or by a fine not exceeding fifty pounds, at the discretion of the court before which he shall be tried ; and any person offending against the provisions of this act in Scotland shall, upon being duly convicted of such offence, be punished by imprisonment for a term not exceeding three months, or by a fine not exceeding fifty pounds, at the discretion of the court before which he shall be tried.*

19. *And in order to remove doubts as to the meaning of certain words in this act, be it enacted, that the words 'person and party' shall be respectively deemed to include any number of persons, or any society, whether by charter or otherwise; and the meaning of the aforesaid words shall not be restricted, although the same may be subsequently referred to in the singular number and masculine gender only.*

The lengths to which the government would now go to ensure that the medical schools received a rigorously controlled supply of corpses is apparent in the above paragraphs, as are the rules and regulations which would soon see the distasteful trade of the resurrectionist being made largely untenable.

It is in the human nature to wonder what was in the paragraphs that were repealed in the House of Commons, and it is reasonable to surmise that these were removed in order to slightly ease the new legislation, which would now govern some of the most powerful men in the country. However, a war had been won, and no longer would the people of Great Britain need to fear their fate after death, at least not in a physical sense.

The crimes of the working class (as were most resurrectionists) had been curtailed by the strict and largely unbreakable governance levied upon their upper class paymasters; something which was very much a first for the British government in the nineteenth century, and is rare even today!

Part 3 – Belt and Braces

In the interim period between the rise of the resurrectionists, and the passing of the Anatomy Act, many communities had felt the need to introduce obstacles and barriers in an attempt to hinder the clandestine digging of the nocturnal body snatchers. Many such preventative measures simply employed the use of night watchmen to patrol the graveyards during the hours of darkness, but, as money was scarce and wages could not always be paid by the local communities, the solution was sometimes found in the most ingenious ideas.

We have already heard of one such method in the case of Hannah Keeson, the young girl whose body was taken from Whitkirk, near Leeds. Unfortunately, the work required to ensure the success of this tactic was not carried out sufficiently in this case, but the theory behind the method was as simple as it was effective in most cases. The adding of straw to the soil which filled the grave was a common method of deterring the resurrection men, as these layers would be compacted by the weight of the soil, especially if the soil was damp, and render the straw almost impenetrable to the body snatcher's shovel, or at least hinder progress so that the task could not be completed within the time available. Another benefit of this was that no expense would be necessary, as straw was as common as soil, especially in the farming communities of rural Britain, and the only investment required was the time and effort taken to build up the alternate layers; something which was not afforded to the grieving family of Hannah Keeson.

Another method which could be implemented without cost was the formation of 'Watch Clubs' in which members of the community were duty bound to do their bit for the town or village, and take turns to wander the graveyards at night, before being relieved by another of their townsfolk. This was an effective deterrent in rural, close-knit communities, but was difficult to organise in the more populous areas, as the graveyards were much bigger, and the sense of community was simply not comparable to that of the rural settlements. Naturally, there would be more people to take their turn on patrol, but naming and shaming those who did not perform their allotted duty would be much more difficult!

Those places that could afford to invest in defences against the resurrectionists found that iron and stone were invaluable in protecting their former loved ones. Sometimes, a method as simple as raising the height of a perimeter wall could be extremely effective, especially if the wall also bore a number of sharp iron spikes on which a body snatcher could become painfully impaled! One of the most popular safeguards was known as a 'mortsafe' (examples of which can still be seen around the country today), which was a cast iron skeleton-like structure, similar to a cage, which was built over a grave, and proved to be the nemesis of many a grave robber in the churches in which these were in operation. Another method was to build an observation tower, from which the sexton, caretaker or groundskeeper could keep a vigilant eye over the consecrated ground in their charge. Many of these buildings are also still in existence, and stand to attention over several historic graveyards across the UK.

As simple as most of these ideas were, it is also worth noting that some amateur inventors went to great lengths in patenting their eccentric, and usually ridiculous, designs; one such idea being the 'spring loaded cemetery cannon' (four words which one would never expect to find in the same sentence). This involved setting a series of tripwires across the churchyard or cemetery, which would trigger explosions from all angles should an intruder find themselves entangled in the trap. However, it is safe to assume that the reason this particular anonymous inventor did not become a millionaire, is that fact that the victim was often a grieving relative, or innocent bystander, who had simply fancied an evening visit to pay their respects to a loved one!

Simpler ideas included the incorporation of wide metal beams into the grave, which would reach further outwards beneath the ground than the grave itself, and thus render the removal of a body very difficult, even if the determined digger had been successful in reaching the casket to begin with. Also, burying the body with the feet closest to the headstone was experimented with, as many resurrection men would dig at the top of the grave, and break open the casket just enough to wrestle the body free by the head and shoulders. However, this was never really a serious deterrent, as any body snatcher who had taken the effort to dig six feet into the earth, would probably not be deterred by being greeted by a pair of feet where a head should be, and would simply drag the body from the ground using the ankles, which would add minutes to the procedure at worst.

Sadly, many could not afford to offer even the merest protection to their lost relatives and loved ones, and as such, could only place an item upon the grave, so they could at least identify if the final resting place of their loved ones had been desecrated or tampered with.

Whatever the method, the main aim was to cause as much nuisance to the resurrection men as they had caused to the community. The population had simply had enough of the nocturnal body thieves, and would gladly put their time and effort into anything which would ensure that the rewards which could be obtained for their loved ones would never be collected.

Yet, the Anatomy Act was eventually the saviour of the day, and put many minds at ease across the nation, apart from that of the man who invented, and subsequently patented, the 'spring loaded cemetery cannon'.

Chapter 9

Lies and Legends

'Everything has got a moral, if only you can find it.'

Lewis Carroll – Alice in Wonderland

Part 1 – Stumbling in the Dark

It is apparent from the cases we have studied in this book, that the on-going threat of disinterment and desecration was a very real concern to the Yorkshire folk of the early to mid-nineteenth century, therefore, it can be of no surprise to learn that many of the incidents that did not make it into the main body of the book, were either of a more trivial nature, or simply untrue.

The first of these minor cases takes place in Sheffield, a city which took a little longer than others to cast off the spectre of the resurrectionists, mainly due to the medical schools which operated in the area, and the unfortunate incidents at Wardsend Cemetery, which provided one of the very last body snatching scandals recorded in the UK. However, our first tale is set far over the horizon of the city and takes place in an outlying area of Sheffield, now treasured as a rural retreat, but historically home to a handful of farms and tiny villages, exactly the kind of place where the resurrectionists found easy pickings. Yet, the perpetrator in this story was not a hardened and desensitised professional, and his carrying out of the macabre task to which he had committed himself was far from being the quick and silent operation one would have expected from our previous examples.

The parish of Bradfield is one of South Yorkshire's most idyllic spots. Split by a steep hill into the separate villages of High Bradfield and Low Bradfield, the lower portion nestles quietly next to the Damflask reservoir, although at the time of this particular tale, the reservoir had yet to be constructed. Given the lack of urban conveniences and its general tranquillity, it is hard to believe that Bradfield is actually one of the largest parishes in the country, its borders taking in the edge of Sheffield, and reaching deep into the adjoining Peak District. Reaching out to the west, the parish is home to the borders of two counties, accommodating both Yorkshire and Derbyshire within its boundaries, which also lay claim to the areas of Stocksbridge, and the Upper Derwent Valley.

However, our story is based in Bradfield itself, and concerns a rare and shameful incident of opportunistic crime, something almost unimaginable in this leafy and panoramic corner of the Sheffield of today's world. On any given Sunday, one can wander into Low Bradfield and see a game of cricket being played at the village clubhouse, and enjoy an ice cream whilst taking in a leisurely walk around the picturesque and unapologetically English scenery. Very little would have been different in the early 1800s. The tiny post office would have been in operation, and the main street would have been as quiet and free from the hustle of city life as it is today. The only difference would have been where the reservoir now stands, which would have been an area of rich and verdant farmland, where much of the local produce would have been reared and nurtured.

However, our tale takes place in High Bradfield, a short, yet gruelling walk from its lower counterpart, taking in a steep and winding country lane, which will test the stamina of even the fittest of walkers. In fact, such is the gradient of the hill, it was used as part of the 2014 Tour de France, and was one of the most testing hill climbs to be included in the route. This inclusion in the world famous event has led to several signs around the village bearing the name 'Cote de Bradfield'.

The upper portion of Bradfield is still home to a number of terraced houses, all of which take pride in their historic roots, and display some of the prettiest gardens that can be found for many a mile. The residents always seem happy to see visitors to the village peering at the vivid colours of the flowers they have so lovingly cultivated. The view from the top of the hill over the Loxley Valley is awe-inspiring, and challenges any visitor to the area to drag themselves away from the majestic and sweeping panorama that stretches out in front of them like a curtain of the brightest green, draped as far as the eye can see.

Pre-dating everything in the village, apart from the view, is the historical Church of St Nicholas, which dominates the brow of the hill with its majestic architecture and extensive grounds, suggesting that the picturesque village was deliberately created around the church. Standing at 260m above sea level, there can be very few churches which boast such a view from their grounds, and even fewer that can claim the peacefulness and quiet tranquillity that still remain today. The present-day church was built in 1480, although a smaller place of worship stood upon the site from the twelfth century, built by the Normans who regarded this part of Yorkshire as an area of strategic importance. In fact, the area was regarded to be of such importance that a motte and bailey castle was built after the Norman Conquest, the ruins of which now lie beneath the houses that adjoin the present day church. The fifteenth century building that we find today was built in the Gothic style, which adds a sense of grandeur and foreboding to those who pass its historic walls, which were painstakingly built using the gritstone of the local area.

Unfortunately, by the time of our story, the church itself had been widely altered by the Puritans in the wake of the English Civil War. The decorative stained glass and wall paintings had all been sanitised by a cover of whitewash, and the statues which graced the interior had been removed. It was not until the late nineteenth century that these changes were reversed, and the building was restored to its former glory. By this time however, the grounds of the church had also been targeted by an act of heinous opportunism, but one that ended more innocuously than any of our previous examples.

It was one o'clock in the morning on 6 February, 1820, when a local resident knocked upon the door of the sexton, Charles Greaves, and reported a suspicious presence in the churchyard. The witness claimed to have heard a series of scraping noises and quiet profanities, which came from behind some of the tall headstones. Had it not been for the ungodly vocabulary of the mysterious man amongst the graves, the sexton could have been forgiven for dismissing the scraping noses as being those made by the sheep, which regularly grazed upon the land, as they still do so today.

Immediately grabbing a lamp and heading for the churchyard, Greaves was alerted to the sound of more than one voice, yet, as the beam of his lantern appeared around the corner of the church, the hushed voices were replaced by swift footsteps retreating in the distance. The scraping nose continued, and it was with great surprise that Greaves could now make out the head and shoulders of a man who seemed to be buried from the chest down. However, the glimpse of the shovel, which rhythmically appeared over the man's shoulder in time with the scraping, and the dirt that flew behind, now gave context to the strange sight that had greeted Mr Greaves. Owing to the sound of the digging, the man in the ground had obviously not heard the approaching sexton and carried on with his work, unaware that his accomplices had deserted him at the first sight of trouble – yet another example of the lack of fraternity often displayed by resurrection men.

Spotting the oncoming light with just seconds to spare before the sexton, who was now joined by the man who had alerted him, descended upon him, the shadowy figure struggled from his hole, and began to make his getaway over a small wall, and into the field beyond. As he ran, the man seemed to throw several bulky objects from the inside of his long coat, and with each new jettison seemed to pick up pace. He was no match for the unburdened men who were hot on his tail however, and was brought crashing to the ground less than 60yds from the scene of his crime. With the lamplight cast upon his face, the two men quickly realised that the culprit was a familiar face, not a resident of High Bradfield, but well know around the local area. His name was Joseph Hall, and he showed not one bit of remorse upon his capture, saying 'if you had been ten minutes later, I'd have got it out and been off with it!'

In terms of execution, this attempted act of body snatching was laughably flawed, as it had also been noted that Hall was stupid enough to have parked his horse and cart directly outside the graveyard entrance, not to mention that he had employed two lookouts who had deserted their post at the merest sign of interference. However, the planning of the robbery had been slightly more impressive, as it was soon revealed in the morning light after Hall had been taken into police custody upon the eventual arrival of the local constable, that he had actually attended a number of funerals at this particular church during the past two or three months. When questioned about this, Hall admitted that he had attended the funeral of the deceased, a Mr Joseph Fox, the very afternoon before his attempted snatching of the body, and had decided to act upon this particular body as he had watched the grave being dug, and noticed that a large stone had prevented the gravedigger from reaching the customary 6ft in depth.

Whilst languishing in custody before his appearance before the Assizes, Hall kept his silence as to the identity of his accomplices (a very generous gesture given their cowardly retreat) and the final destination of the corpse had he been successful in his task. This silence continued throughout his very short trial at the Pontefract Sessions, and with no mitigating circumstances to offer, and a wealth of evidence against him, including the tools he had tried to scatter throughout the fields during his attempted getaway, Hall was sentence to six months imprisonment by the deeply unimpressed judge. It is safe to assume that the body would have been offered to the local medical school, or packed onto a coach bound for Edinburgh. But, because of the sheer incompetence of Joseph Hall, the anatomists would have to wait for another specimen to work upon.

Part 2 – Murky Waters

In 1832, a rapidly-travelling cholera epidemic hit the population of the West Riding of Yorkshire after beginning its wake of destruction in the North East. The unwanted arrival was heralded by a lurid newspaper headline, in which the *Leeds Intelligencer* grandly announced that: 'the pestilence has gained a footing in Yorkshire'.

The unfortunate man reported to have been the original source of the epidemic was William Sproat, a keelman from Sunderland, who had allegedly contracted the illness whilst carrying out his duties abroad and at sea. This was certainly an accolade that nobody wanted to be presented with. It was in October 1831 that Sproat succumbed to his illness, just eight months before the deadly disease had spread across the spine of the nation, and taken Yorkshire by force. From the day of Sproat's death, the spread of the disease could be tangibly tracked as it travelled across the area, but with no known cure, nothing could be done to save those who found themselves in its deadly wake. From the onset of his illness, Sproat took just three days to meet his maker. The terrible symptoms of violent vomiting and purging, accompanied by the gut wrenching stomach cramps, left those who had reluctantly attended his bedside with no doubt that this was the work of the Asiatic Cholera.

By the time the *Leeds Intelligencer* had made its proclamation, the disease had struck in Goole, just a short distance away from the 76,000 souls who inhabited the industrial town of Leeds, and those who governed this West Riding settlement were well aware that the sanitation and living conditions within the area were not equipped to cope with an epidemic; if anything, the cholera would be aided by these shortfalls.

Selby was next to fall victim on 15 May, when it was reported that Thomas Hughes, a boatman who regularly crossed the River Ouse to York, had been consumed by the illness and, within ten days, his brother, father, and uncle, had also contracted the disease. This was quickly followed by the neighbours of the Hughes family, who had been using the same outdoor convenience. The day of reckoning finally fell upon Leeds on 28 May, and as the town was so densely populated, 427 cases were reported over the next month – a number that was set to multiply as time went on, and the infection spread between families, work colleagues, and neighbours. The terrible living conditions endured by many of the Leeds residents had long been a source of contention between the townsfolk and the local authorities, and with the added threat of fatal illness, it was not long before the local newspapers began to fan the flames, the *Leeds Mercury* described the centre of Leeds as 'a receptacle of poverty, misery, and uncleanness.'

Spurred on by the negative press, the local authorities decided that now was the time to show willing, and commissioned a report to be made as to the sanitation and living conditions within the town. This was to be overseen by the well-respected District Surgeon, Dr Robert Baker. Unfortunately for the local population, Baker's report would not be completed until many more of the townsfolk had died of cholera. But, in publishing his report (in sections, until it was completed) in the newspapers, the surviving residents were at least aware that the conditions in which they were forced to live were now causing considerable embarrassment to the local authorities.

In one such instalment, which appeared in the Leeds Intelligencer, Dr Baker left no doubt as to his own distaste as to the sights which had greeted him throughout his work, describing the horrors of certain areas of the town with all of the bluntness of a man keen to enforce investment.

Baxter's Yard – most dingy, privies open
Cherry Tree Yard – open privies, very bad
Jack Lane – an offensive ditch nearby
Orange Street – most wretchedly bad
Micklethwaite's Walk – stones have to be put down to walk
Marsh Lane Back – most filthy

Another such observation came as Baker described 'a vast mound of night soil' (human waste) that covered an area of almost 40 sq yds, describing this, almost laughably, as 'a striking monument to civil neglect.'

Over the next year or two, Dr Baker became the social justice warrior so desperately needed to represent the townsfolk. His work took him to other areas of injustice, such as the appalling working conditions of the local industries, to the plight of those who had been placed at the mercy of the Leeds workhouses. However, beneath the public admiration for Dr Baker lay a whispered rumour, one which would soon spread and threaten the reputation of the very man who had been seen as the saviour of Leeds; it was suggested that the work undertaken by the respected doctor was nothing more than a front to cover up more nefarious activities.

It had been noticed that many of the poor souls who breathed their last in the workhouses, which were now under the control of Baker, were simply taken away, never to receive a burial, or to be recorded in any official death certificate. At first, this was treated as idle rumour, but before long, an incident from six years earlier was resurrected (pun intended). During mid-March 1826, it had been reported that the body of a 15-year-old girl, Martha Oddy, had been removed from the churchyard at Armley, after the recently-dug grave was noted to have been disturbed. Upon inspection, this bore all the hallmarks of the resurrection men: the coffin lay empty save for the burial clothes. Two men, Thomas Smith and Michael Armstrong, were eventually arrested for the theft of the body, yet during the subsequent court appearance, it was alleged by Armstrong that he had thought that he was acting on orders from Dr Baker himself, who had, in turn, paid him £4 for the cadaver. This was also confirmed during the testimony of Thomas Smith. Yet, no evidence existed to confirm this serious allegation against one of the town's top officials, and no action was ever taken against Dr Baker, who kept his silence on the subject and allowed the two allegedly hired men to face their punishment without feeling the need to make any statement of explanation. The whispered rumours were to follow Baker throughout his career, yet even during the period in which the bodies of the poor seemed to disappear into the ether, which handily coincided with the opening of the Leeds Medical School, no further action was ever taken against the good doctor, a man who had been instrumental in improving the facilities of the town for the poor and needy. It is not beyond the reach of imagination to examine these occurrences and decide that some macabre work was being undertaken by Baker, as his close ties with the new medical school and the local workhouses would provide ample opportunity for him to make a few extra pounds for his troubles. However, we must assume innocence until proof is available, and so Dr Baker will be remembered as the man who cleaned up a town, and left a legacy of improved sanitation, better workplaces, and did his duty to the sick and destitute.

It should also be noted that, aside from the disinterment of Martha Oddy, the acts in which Baker was rumoured to be involved were not illegal. The supply of corpses from the workhouses to the medical schools *was* allowed, but had this ever been proven, the city, which Baker helped to rebuild, could have easily been reduced to rubble once more, by the hands of those he sought to help.

Part 3 – A Mix-Up at the Morgue

Having read the unforgettable tale of the Wardsend Riot, it would seem that Sheffield was still haunted by the threat of the resurrectionists long after the rest of the county was sleeping soundly in the knowledge that they would, one day, be able to rest in peace. However, the nationwide scandal caused by the riot was not to be the end of dubious occurrences that would take place within the city.

Our final tale actually took place as late as 1882, a time when the country was beginning to make vast leaps forwards in social advancement and medical progress. Yet, as will become clear, the tale of John Wood raises many questions as to the validity of these advancements. Could the illicit supply of corpses have been taking place as late as 1882?

This particular incident came to the attention of the press due to a hastily arranged enquiry, which had been prompted in light of an especially large 'mistake', which had been made by a funeral parlour situated in the city centre. However, as will become apparent, to call this incident 'a mistake' may be extremely generous, especially as this dubious choice of noun seems to absolve all involved of any wrongdoing, something which could only be achieved by a huge stretch of the imagination.

The enquiry was held in a private room of the Sheffield Workhouse, a large stone building close to Kelham Island. Present were representatives of the workhouse, the funeral parlour in question, an extremely annoyed widow, and Mr Basil Cane, the Poor Law Inspector, who fulfilled the role of chairman. Also crammed into the draughty room was a select handful of reporters. Many more had arrived on that morning, rumoured to have been tipped off by one of the parties involved, but just a few were granted permission to be present at the meeting. The room hushed as Mr Cane began to read out the report, which he had meticulously produced in the wake of this bizarre incident. The story, as told by Mr Cane, and which appeared in the *Sheffield Independent*, is printed in its entirety below:

Mr. Basil Cane, Poor Law Inspector held an enquiry at the Sheffield Workhouse yesterday concerning the removal of the body of a young man named John Wood which was taken by mistake to the Medical School instead of that of an old man named Ellis.

Wood, it appeared, had been received into the hospital suffering from consumption and died within ten minutes of his admission. On the widow coming to claim the body for burial she was shown a coffin on which was a plate bearing the name of 'John Wood age 36'.

On the lid being removed, however, she found that the coffin did not contain Wood's body but that of an old man named Ellis. Search was made and Wood's body was ultimately found lying on a slab at the Medical School ready for the anatomical lecturer and his students.

Mrs. Wood declared that when the body was brought back to the workhouse there were several cuts to the neck as if inflicted by a lancet. It was explained that the cuts had been inflicted by the porter at the school in the process of shaving.

The mistake arose through the recent appointment of a new man to take charge of the dead-house, and the failure to put cards bearing the names and ages on the bodies

Clearly, several questions are immediately raised by this phenomenal series of events. Firstly, and most importantly, why was it only when Mrs Wood asked for the coffin to be opened that any question was raised as to the occupant of the casket? Surely, it would be prudent to check that the right corpse had been sent to the medical school? Or could this be a case of the funeral parlour and the workhouse putting their heads together in order to make a few pounds? First, it would have been quite easy to swap the intended body for a younger, healthier one, thus increasing the value of the deal. All that was required was to bury the intended corpse in place of the younger one, and nobody would be any the wiser, unless, of course, a relative insisted on the coffin being opened for their own inspection.

Second, even if the story about the new employee at the funeral parlour failing to label the bodies correctly was true, how could anyone mistake the body of a 36-year-old man, for that of an elderly and malnourished man, fresh from the workhouse? One would imagine that, given the fate of one of the bodies (sadly due to poverty and low social standing) was very different from that which was intended for the other. To send a man, whose family had paid for a funeral, to the dissection table must be something for which a funeral parlour would prepare correctly.

And finally, if the cadaver sent to the medical school had been cut during a posthumous shave, one must really question why a body that was about to be dissected would be given a makeover? As many would no doubt suspect, the marks on the neck would have been made by a scalpel in the preliminary moments of a dissection, and could hardly be confused with a few shaving nicks caused by a careless attendant.

This may be no more than educated conjecture, but many would hazard a guess that the parties involved had seen the opportunity to provide a higher quality cadaver than originally intended, something which the medical school would no doubt have welcomed. The tenacity of Mrs Wood had not been accounted for however, and by the time the correct body had been located, the dissection had already begun, explaining the marks upon the neck of the late John Wood.

The outcome of the enquiry was eventually nothing more than a slap on the wrists for all involved; yet the real punishment would no doubt have come in the form of trial by press. The majority of the people of Sheffield had not yet forgotten the event of Wardsend Cemetery, and it was highly unlikely that the participants in this little comedy of errors would be allowed to forget their own indiscretions. One major positive aspect that did arise from the ashes of this farce, was that the press began to question the use of cadavers from the workhouses for dissection, something of which the unfortunate, and, sadly, unnamed elderly gentleman, who almost received a proper funeral, would have been proud.

Part 4 – A Very Brief Mention of Alexander Lyons

As a parting gift, and something to lighten the mood a little, I give you the darkly comedic tale of Alexander Lyons, a man who was known to be part of the Sheffield resurrection trade, but was, unfortunately, not in possession of the 'full shilling'.

Lyons was suspected of having been involved in several body snatching incidents, but as his intellect was seemingly even lower than his morals, he was usually put to use as a lookout, or hired muscle to be charged with the duties of lugging heavy boxes through the streets and into the back entrances of the medical schools. A huge young man, whom many described as 'harmless' and 'daft as a brush', Lyons eventually tired of making a few pennies for his role in these lucrative businesses, and took the unwise decision to set out in business on his own.

However, young Lyons would never complete his solo jaunt into the murky world of the body snatcher. In the end, it would be the simplest of mistakes that would give the game away, one which would even bring laughter from the magistrate during his eventual court appearance. Having participated in more than a few nocturnal escapades, Lyons was quite well drilled in the necessary procedures and, being as strong as an ox, would not require any assistance in hauling his bounty from the earth unaided. He had even managed to stake out a funeral the previous afternoon, and had wisely selected a victim whose earthly remains were sure to fetch the top price at the medical school but, having succeeded in single-handedly doing the heavy, back-breaking work of digging out his intended prey, Lyons realised that he had forgotten something.

Having decided to work alone, and having also travelled to the graveyard on foot, the calamitous Lyons realised with a start that he had not made any provision for removing the body from the graveyard. He had no sack, no box, and no ideas. Yet it was not long before the unique mind of Alexander Lyons arrived at a conclusion. He would forgo the traditional horse and cart, and walk into town with the newly resurrected cadaver, whilst simply acting as if nothing were amiss. So, as one would expect to see in a Carry On film or comedy sketch, Lyons secured the leg of the corpse around his own with a length of rope, and placed his arm around the shoulder of his new friend. Surely nobody would question two close friends taking a night-time stroll together?

With a mind full of optimism, and dreaming of how he would spend the handsome fee, Lyons and his late walking partner began their bizarre wander towards the gas lamps of the city centre, with Lyons even having the forethought to engage his companion in conversation whenever any other person was nearby. Incredibly, this audacious tactic almost worked, and this macabre three-legged race was not to be drawn to a halt until well in sight of the medical school where, to the dismay of Lyons, a puzzled police constable was eyeing this unusual sight with a mix of understandable trepidation and keen interest in what was occurring immediately before him. Having recognised Lyons at once, and being aware of his questionable trade, the constable quickly put two and two together, and (no doubt suppressing a grin), went over to engage the two men in conversation.

Knowing that the game was up if he could not pull another iron out of the fire, Lyons greeted the constable cheerily, and tried to carry on walking towards his destination. However, the policeman would not be put off so easily, and enquired as to the identity of Lyons' new friend. With a sharpness of mind that very few would have expected from this young man, Lyons quickly explained to the constable that his friend was 'extremely drunk' and that he wanted to get him home as soon as possible. But the game was up and the only person still believing the story was Lyons himself.

Sounding his whistle, and soon being accompanied by three more constables, the policeman smilingly relieved Lyons of his burden, and ensured that his colleagues had secured the mighty limbs of the erstwhile body snatcher before removing the body to the police station, from where it would be taken to the graveyard and finally laid to rest the next morning.

Happily, despite the serious offence he had committed, the punishment in store for Lyons was not too severe, and he escaped with just a few weeks imprisonment during which he could think about what he had done and, as far as anyone is aware, he never returned to the resurrection business again.

As for the family of the resurrected man, one can only assume that they were extremely upset by the whole business, but it would be comforting to imagine that, once the dust had settled down, they also allowed themselves a wry smile at the stupidity of Alexander Lyons!

Historia est Vitae Magistra
(History is the Tutor of life)

Walkley, Sheffield, July 2016

As creation of this compendium is complete (save for the final flourishes), I finally have a chance to sit back and reflect upon the dark world that has been my late night companion for the last nine months. It is very easy in this day and age to find yourself to be desensitised to death and misery, as long as it is in the past. Yet, as with many of the tragic events that have unfolded during the first half of this calendar year, one can only imagine that there is some corner of the world where the misery I have described to you upon these pages, is very real and very recent.

The passing of a loved one is always difficult, but in our safe, modern, western world, one cannot even begin to comprehend the pain of burying a family member, only to discover that even their last resting place was anything but a place of peace. Therefore, it is very important to not only imagine the murky settings and disreputable characters featured in these tales, but to also imagine the human feeling that is almost impossible as a writer to capture by means of words on paper.

Now that my work is (almost) complete, I find myself thinking about the real people featured in this book, and how their lives were to continue beyond the end of their respective chapters. The resurrection men themselves are largely irrelevant, as they were just men who chose a dishonourable path in order to provide themselves with a means to live in a time and location where money was scarce, and life was, unfortunately, cheap.

It is the victims of this foul trade that deserve to be remembered. The twice-bereaved Mr Bagshawe, who lost his child and his wife within days of each other, only to be informed that the body of his beloved son had been taken by opportunistic thieves. One can only hope that he found some kind of solace in years to come. Likewise, the despairing family of young Hannah Keeson, so cruelly taken away by illness during an extremely harsh winter, only to be removed from the place of rest that her family had selected in the local graveyard, with the intention of keeping her close to home.

Also to be remembered, are the families who descended upon cemeteries in Barnsley and Sheffield, frantically digging at the cold earth with their bare hands in order to ascertain whether their loved ones still lay in the consecrated ground, or had long since been victim to the scalpels of the anatomists.

Another footnote to this compendium is an apology, or rather an offer of an apology, as many of the stories featured in this book contain the details of allegations which, in reality, were no more than rumours. The intentions and actions of many learned men have been called into question, although not without a certain amount of circumstantial evidence, but should these rumours have been untrue, and these pillars of society have played no part in the macabre tales with which they have been linked, then my sincerest apologies go out to their memories, and their existing families.

It would be a lie to report that I wrote this book without ever raising a wry smile; I did so on many occasions. However, these moments of black comedy always seemed to come when writing about the capture of the resurrectionists; often due to the mistakes and gaffes that even the most experienced body snatchers seemed to make on a regular basis. The final tale of the final chapter, the story of Alexander Lyons, had me in stitches from start to finish, not because I have no sense of the pain felt by the family of the victim, but because it is a genuinely funny story, and was a pleasure to end the compendium with.

I will also admit that I will not be sorry to be relieved of wandering around graveyards in the rain, searching forlornly for a headstone which has long since been removed, or has simply eroded due to the ravages of time. The research of this book has cost me at least two pairs of shoes, consigned to the bin as unrecognisable lumps of sodden mud. It also cost me my tolerance of sheep, after one particularly savage biting incident whilst taking photographs at High Bradfield. Yet, I can honestly say that it has all been worth it, and I am proud to have uncovered stories that had slipped from the history books, and become all but lost in the realm of local folklore. There are still monuments to commemorate some of the larger scale incidents in this book, and I would urge you to visit them if you have chance.

Yorkshire is a fascinating region with a whole world of forgotten stories ready to be uncovered and brought into the light once more. I only hope that this offering has piqued a little sense of adventure in every reader, and that many more of you will take the opportunity to look into the past for inspiration.

Finally, as I contemplate turning off the computer and heading to bed, I would like to finish by thanking everybody who has supported me by buying a copy of this book; or by recommending and lending it to a friend. I'm well aware that Yorkshire folk aren't made of money! Thank you for continually supporting my work, and for giving me the opportunity to keep on delving into the dark recesses of this wonderful county, a county which I am extremely proud to call home.

PS. If you ever pay a visit to the churchyard at High Bradfield, please make sure that you don't have any food in your pockets, as the livestock which roam this beautiful part of the world have fewer morals than any of the resurrection men featured in this book.

Ben Johnson

Bibliography

Books

Peach. H, *Curious Tales of Old North Yorkshire*, Sigma Press 2003

Drinkall. M, *19th Century Barnsley Murders*, Pen and Sword Local History 2015

Sharpe. J, *Dick Turpin; the Myth of the English Highwayman*, Profile Books 2005

Baring-Gould. S, *Yorkshire Oddities, Incidents and Strange Events, Volume 2*, General Books 2010

Dudley-Edwards. O, *Burke and Hare*, Birlinn Ltd 2014

Wise. S, *The Italian Boy: Murder and Grave-Robbery in 1830s London*, Pimlico 2005

Richardson. R, *Death, Dissection and the Destitute*, University of Chicago Press 2000

Newspapers and Periodicals

Read's Weekly Journal, 8 February, 1735

Gentleman's Magazine, June edition, 1737

The Illustrated Edinburgh News, 26 December, 1828

Newry Telegraph, 31 March, 1829

The Hull and Eastern Counties Herald, 2 January 1829

Sheffield Independent, 1 February 1829, 27 January 1835, 8 June 1862, 12 August 1870, 18 March 1882

The Leeds Intelligencer, 16 May 1831

Leeds Patriot and Yorkshire Advertiser, 10 November 1831

The Lancet - Volume 19, August 1832

The Times, 9 June 1862

Online Resources

www.opendomesday.org

www.britannica.com

www.leodis.net

www.historyofyork.org.uk

www.archive.org

www.history.co.uk

www.britishexecutions.co.uk

www.weirdisland.co.uk

www.york-united-kingdom.co.uk

www.picturesheffield.com

www.mediafiles.thedms.co.uk
www.historytoday.com
www.kingscollections.org
www.lookandlearn.com
www.chrishobbs.com
www.bl.uk
www.sciencemuseum.org.uk
www.geograph.org.uk
www.historyhouse.co.uk
www.peakdistrictinformation.com
www.jstor.org
www.britainsforgottenbodysnatchers.blogspot.com
www.picssr.com
www.redbubble.com
www.writingfamilyhistory.com
www.alamy.com
www.artuk.org
www.southyorkshirethroughtime.org.uk
www.sheffieldtimewalk.wordpress.com
www.murderpedia.org
www.britishlibrary.typepad.co.uk
www.mtg-realm.blogspot.com
www.historyofbiologyandmedicine.com
www.capitalpunishmentuk.org
www.cutlers-hallamshire.org.uk

Index